Productivity in the Local Government Sector

Productivity in the Local Government Sector

John P. Ross
Virginia Polytechnic Institute
and State University
Jesse Burkhead
Syracuse University

Lexington Books
D.C. Heath and Company
Lexington, Massachusetts
Toronto   London

Library of Congress Cataloging in Publication Data

Ross, John P.   1943-
    Productivity in the local government sector.

    Bibliography: p.
    1. Local government—United States. 2. Labor productivity—United
States. I. Burkhead, Jesse, joint author. II. Title.
JS363.R67   352'.005'147   74-13900
ISBN 0-669-94763-6

Published simultaneously in Canada.

Printed in the United States of America.

International Standard Book Number: 0-669-94763-6

Library of Congress Catalog Card Number: 74-13900

Preface

This volume originated in a research project in the summer and fall of 1971 conducted by Seymour Sacks and myself for the New York State Temporary Commission on the Powers of Local Government (the Wagner Commission). We were asked by the commission to explore changes in local government expenditures in New York State for the 1959-69 period; our findings were filed with the commission in December 1971 and were incorporated in their final report. We are indebted to the commission for the initial financing of this research.

As a part of this project, Ross and I undertook an exploration of research in government productivity and encountered the cost-workload-scope and quality approach that had been used by other public finance economists. This suggested a useful and operational approach to this complex problem, and we enlisted the help of Polly A. Burkhead, Assistant Professor of Mathematics, LeMoyne College, who developed the model in Chapter 5. We were also greatly assisted at this stage by comments and suggestions from Robert D. Reischauer, The Brookings Institution; Selma Mushkin, Georgetown University; Harry Hatry and Harold Hochman, The Urban Institute; Robert Lindsay, The New York State Council of Economic Advisors; and Jerry Kelly, Department of Economics, Syracuse University.

Ross subsequently joined the staff of the Ohio Commission on Local Government Services where he prepared the materials in Chapters 1, 2, 3, and 4.

Our first draft materials benefited from the comments of Seymour Sacks and others on the project staff: Donna Shalala, Bernard Jump, David Bjornstad, Paul O'Farrell, and Jerry Wade. Subsequent comments and suggestions from Roy Bahl and John Henning, Department of Economics, Syracuse University were also most helpful.

Financial support for the final revision was provided by a grant from the Ford Foundation for a study of local government employment. This volume is, in part, the first product of this project. The final revisions also benefited from the comments of Stan Czamanski, editor of this series for Lexington Books.

Secretarial staffs assume a particularly heavy burden for the typing and retyping of academic manuscripts. In this instance, these include Virginia Halsey and Leslie Sanders, Department of Economics, Syracuse University; Kay Cesser and Linda Stewart, Ohio Commission on Local Government Services; and John C. Hollwitz and Phyllis Perrine, Metropolitan Studies Program, Syracuse University.

As this volume has evolved, we now feel that it may serve two useful purposes. First, it is a report on the "state of the art" in the difficult and complex field of public sector productivity analysis—a field of inquiry in which we anticipate there will be growing interest. Second, the model that is developed in Chapter 5 and tested in Chapter 6 is, we believe, an operationally useful contribution for academic inquiry, but also, and particularly a contribution for local government budget officers and systems analysts who are responsible for the staff work that contributes to a more responsible and responsive system of local government service delivery.

Jesse Burkhead

Productivity in the Local
Government Sector

1　Introduction

One of the most significant phenomena occurring in the United States economy today is the rapid growth of the public sector. Tables 1-1 and 1-2 indicate the relative and absolute growth that has occurred in public sector goods and service expenditures and employment between 1962 and 1972. Total public sector expenditures have increased by more than 100 percent while public employment increased by almost 50 percent. The public sector's relative growth is less impressive. In 1962 public sector goods and service expenditures made up about 21 percent of gross national product, whereas by 1972 they accounted for 22 percent of GNP. Public sector expenditures as a percentage of GNP grew at an average annual rate of 0.6 percent, while public sector employment as a percentage of total nonagricultural wage and salary workers grew at a rate of 4.1 percent per year.

Although this growth has occurred in all parts of the public sector, it has occurred more rapidly at the state and local level than at the national level. During this period, federal government expenditures increased by about 65 percent, while expenditures of state and local governments increased by about 180 percent. Federal government employment grew at a rate of 1.2 percent per year, while state and local government employment grew at an average annual rate of 5.1 percent. These changes in both expenditure and employment make state and local government one of the fastest growing sectors of the economy. And this impressive growth is predicted to continue, although at a slower pace, over the next decade.

The factors contributing to this growth are much easier to describe than they are to measure. If asked to identify the principal factor causing local public sector growth, most economists would point to increasing urbanization. As urbanization continues, social overhead capital requirements increase. Transportation networks must be expanded. Water and sewerage facilities must be enlarged. Additional recreational facilities must be constructed as living density increases. By increasing the quantity and intensity of interaction among people, urbanization both expands and intensifies the number of externalities with which local governments must deal. In some cases these externalities can be corrected by regulation. In others, additional local government expenditures are required, as with traffic congestion. Market failures in urbanized areas often generate additional needs for public sector activity, as in the provision of an adequate supply of low-income housing. This and other failures have added increased pressures for local public-sector expenditures.

1

Table 1-1

Public Sector Expenditures (In Billions)

	1962	1972	Percentage Increase	Annual Rate of Growth
GNP	$560.3	$1,115.2	106.2	7.5
Total Public Sector	117.1	255.0	117.8	8.1
Federal Government	63.4	104.5	64.8	5.1
State and Local Government	53.7	150.5	180.3	10.9
Total Public Sector as a Percentage of GNP	20.9	22.1	5.7	0.6
Federal Government as a Percentage of GNP	11.3	9.0	−20.4	− 2.0
State and Local Government as a Percentage of GNP	9.6	13.0	35.4	3.1

Source: Data from *Economic Report of the President* (Washington, D.C.: U.S. Government Printing Office, 1974) p. 249. Public expenditures include only goods and service payments; transfers are omitted.

Table 1-2

Employment: Wage and Salary Workers in Nonagricultural Establishments (In Thousands)

	1962	1972	Percentage Increases	Annual Rate of Growth
Total	55,596	72,764	31.1	2.7
Total Public	8,890	13,290	49.5	4.1
Federal	2,340	2,650	13.2	1.2
State and Local	6,550	10,640	62.4	5.1
Total Public as Percentage of Total	16.0	18.3	14.4	1.4
Federal as Percentage of Total	4.2	3.6	−14.3	−1.4
State and Local as Percentage of Total	11.8	14.6	23.7	2.1

Source: Data from *Economic Report of the President* (Washington, D.C.: U.S. Government Printing Office, 1974), p. 282.

Economists also point to the income elasticity of both the demand for public services and the tax revenue used to support those services. The income elasticity of demand for public services is certainly greater than 1. A 1 percent increase in income will generate an increase in demand for public services of more than 1 percent. For many local governments, revenue elasticity is less than unity; for the federal government and some state and local governments, the overall elasticity is greater than 1. Since expenditures do to some extent depend upon revenues, the result in these latter cases is an increase in government activity as income rises.

Description of these factors is important, but it does not provide the kinds of answers to taxpayer questions about his local government when he is asked to vote an increase in property-tax millage to support schools or asked to vote a new bond issue for a rapid transit system. The taxpayer wants to know why these increases are necessary. Is he receiving more services? Has the quality of his services improved? Is he getting his money's worth from the government?[1] In other words, how efficiently is his government operating?

On the whole, economic analysis has not been able to provide satisfactory answers to these questions, for quite legitimate reasons. The major difficulty is simply the inability to define and measure the quantity and quality of public sector outputs. The pure theory of public finance, the obvious place to look for answers in this area, rests upon the distinction between private and public goods. The latter are those characterized by the qualities of nonexclusion and nonrivalry. For such goods, the concept of a unit of output is rather ambiguous and, operationally, direct pricing is impossible. Of course, products provided by local governments are not pure public goods in the strict sense, but most of them do display some degree of "publicness." Most are also services, and services by nature are perishable. They expire in the act of performance, leaving the economist with no physical unit of output that may be counted. Since many publicly supplied services are financed from general taxes, the economist does not even have a price dimension with which to work. Lacking these two dimensions, identification and estimation of supply and demand relationships for publicly provided services has proved to be extremely difficult. It is almost impossible to identify benefits at the margin with changes in quantity or quality characteristics on the demand side and cost at the margin with changes in factor inputs on the supply side. The result has been a blurring of output and outcomes or consequences on the demand side, and a blurring of the production process with the product on the supply side.

Discussions of economic efficiency are usually confined to the general framework of production theory. At the very heart of production theory is the concept of the production function, a general relationship between inputs and outputs. Defining such a function for public sector services has proved to be very difficult. The definition of such a relationship requires a unit of output. It also requires the assumption that the public manager is aware of marginal products and strives for least-cost input combinations. Yet public managers are probably not aware of the marginal products of their input factors. And even if they are aware, least-cost input combinations may not be achievable because of the institutional parameters within which they must operate.

Finally, local government public sector analysis must face the frustrating problem of inadequate data. Most local governments simply do not collect the kinds of information necessary for an analysis of input-output relationships. And those that do have only recently begun to keep such data on a systematic basis.

Despite these analytical problems, local government expenditures continue to rise and taxpayers continue to demand direct answers to their questioning of government performance. The purpose of this volume is to develop and test a method for analyzing changes in local government expenditures that will isolate the components of those changes attributable to cost, workload, and quality and productivity. The overall goal of this work is to provide a method for helping to answer some of those persistent taxpayer questions regarding the performance of their local governments.

The Importance of Local
Government Productivity

There are many reasons for examining local government productivity. Probably the most important one is to answer the taxpayer's questions regarding the use of his tax dollar. In a discussion of local government productivity, Edward K. Hamilton recently wrote that

the public is now assailed by more irrelevant facts, half facts, and non-facts on this subject than on any issue in public affairs. For too long, the citizen has been forced to rely for his productivity judgments on the whims, the impressions, and the often uninformed opinion of public spokesmen innocent of any real knowledge of the workings of government.[2]

Thus any study which removes some of these "irrelevant facts, half facts, and non-facts," and in the process better equips the citizen to evaluate his local government, is well worth the effort.

Second, the ability to partition changes in expenditure into its component parts will improve public sector management. It will allow local governments to improve their planning for future needs. Areas of high and low productivity can be identified and appropriate action taken. Cities performing a particular function very efficiently can be identified and some of their techniques can be transferred to other jurisdictions.

Finally, measurements of local government productivity will improve aggregate analysis of economic growth. At present the public sector is simply ignored in studies of aggregate productivity. This is because gross national product data, the source of information for most aggregate studies, values public sector output at factor costs. By definition, public sector productivity cannot change, and a rapidly growing sector of the economy is unfortunately omitted from the analysis. As a result, the implications for the whole economy that can be drawn from aggregate productivity studies are limited and sometimes misleading.

One may be ignoring more than just a problem of underestimating or overestimating aggregate productivity by neglecting the public sector. William J. Baumol has suggested that low productivity growth in the public sector is one of the primary reasons for the present urban fiscal crisis. To reach this conclusion, he begins by postulating a two-sector model. One sector contains those economic activities that are technologically progressive; the other those activities that permit "only sporadic increases in productivity." The low-productivity sector includes economic activities which

for all practical purposes the labor is itself the end product.... there are a number of services in which the labor is an end in itself, in which quality is judged directly in terms of amounts of labor.[3]

Unfortunately, most of the services provided by state and local governments fall into the low-productivity sector. Baumol's model rests on two assumptions: first, that wages in the two sectors are tied together and therefore move up and down as one; and second, that wage rates are set in the technologically progressive sector. Given these two assumptions, as output increases, cost per unit will remain constant in the technologically progressive sector but rise rapidly in the nonprogressive sector. If output growth in the two sectors is held in balance, labor will shift from the progressive to the nonprogressive sector. The result of any attempt to achieve balanced growth will be a reduction in the overall rate of economic growth. Combining these predictions with what Baumol termed "the static externalities" of urban living—road crowding, smoke, and so forth—spells disaster for the costs of municipal services. Municipal service costs will tend to increase without limit and there is little if anything that can be done to stop this increase.[4]

"Baumol's disease," as this hypothesis has been named, has disastrous implications for cities. These implications depend upon the assumption that in the provision of public services, productivity has grown relatively slowly, if at all. Although at present this assumption has not been empirically verified, neither has it been contradicted.

Productivity Measurement

Productivity is a relatively simple concept. It is a measure of efficiency usually expressed as the ratio of the quantity of output to the quantity of input used in the production of that output. For the private sector, where a quantifiable unit of output is available, the simplicity of the concept may be illustrated by some elementary arithmetic. Suppose T_0 and T_1 represent the operation of a firm at two points in time.

	Man-hours	Units of Output	Output per Man-hour	Productivity Index
T_0	300	100	0.33	100
T_1	250	100	0.40	121

In these circumstances, labor productivity (assuming no increase in the quantity of capital employed) has increased by 21 percent.

From this simple example, it is evident that the increase in the labor productivity of the firm can be measured with some precision, and there are, in addition, techniques available for assigning a productivity increase to the contributions of labor and capital.

Changes in cost per unit of output may be measured as follows:

	Cost per Unit of Output	Number of Units of Output	Cost Index	Cost Saving
T_0	$3.00	100	100	
T_1	2.50	100	84	$50

Here the decline in the cost per unit from 100 to 84 is a 16 percent cost saving. A productivity increase has been reflected in a cost reduction. The productivity increase, under competitive labor market conditions, would presumably be reflected in upward salary adjustments.[5]

Although the concept itself is simple enough, its use by the popular press, labor unions, and politicians has elevated productivity to the point that it has now become one of those sacred economic goals for the nation to strive for, and which under no circumstances should be questioned. The result is a great deal of popular confusion concerning exactly what productivity means. This confusion has been increased by the multiplicity of methods by which private sector productivity may be measured and by the problems, both theoretical and practical, which still remain to be solved. To clarify some of this confusion, Chapter 2 discusses the concept of productivity, emphasizing its application in the public sector. It also outlines the different measurement techniques and identifies the major theoretical and practical problems still confronting private sector productivity measurement.

As noted above, the ability to measure public sector productivity has been seriously impaired by the lack of adequate estimates of public sector output. Physical homogeneous units of output that may be measured over time simply do not exist. There is no well-defined objective function for most public sector services. Rather, each service reflects a multiplicity of goals. As these goals change over time, it may be argued that public sector output is changing.

Although a number of methods have been suggested for measuring public sector output, even the most cursory review of the literature in this area indicates the degree of confusion and disagreement over the proper unit for analysis. Chapter 3 examines some of those methods, stressing those which are most appropriate for use within the production function framework. In general, all of these methods have serious weaknesses.

Although the difficulties discussed in Chapter 3 have hindered the investigation of public sector productivity, some empirical studies have been done. Chapter 4 reviews these studies, examining first the studies of federal government productivity and then the efforts to measure state and local government productivity.

Like private sector productivity, government productivity may be measured at a number of levels. The concern may be with aggregate or governmentwide productivity. It may be with departmental or bureau productivity. It may concern one or a number of services. The empirical studies of federal government productivity, particularly those concerned with the department or bureau level are promising, but as yet no studies have provided reliable estimates of aggregate federal government productivity. The major problem with all of these studies is the neglect of quality changes. None incorporate a quality adjustment into their estimates of output. Yet on the whole, work in federal government productivity has been advancing and is likely to continue.

The only fact that can be stated with assurance about local government productivity is that little is known. Very little empirical work has been done in this area, and from what has been done no strong conclusions can be drawn. The most recent developments have concentrated on improving rather than measuring local government productivity. Activities or manpower deployment have been examined rather than output. New York City has taken the lead in this approach, and its experience will be briefly reviewed. If anything at all can be concluded from the research that has been done, it is that there seems to be no evidence of increases in local government productivity that approach the gains that have been made in private sector productivity.

Measuring Expenditure Components

Chapter 5 develops a methodology for analyzing changes in local government expenditures. The method assumes that it is possible to examine local public goods within the general framework of a production function while recognizing the difficulties involved in identifying such a function. The approach introduces the concept of *projected value*. An expenditure function based on cost and workload is hypothesized and used to estimate a projected value for expenditures. The difference between actual expenditures and the projected value of expenditures is the residual. It is made up of changes both in the quality of the government service and in the productivity of the governmental unit providing the service.

The next step is to partition the change in expenditure into its cost, workload, and quality and productivity components, isolating the percentage of the change due to each of these factors. Separating quality from productivity changes is the difficult remaining task.

This method concentrates on outputs rather than on activities, thus differing from other recent public sector productivity analysis. It stresses services and is most useful for examining a specific service as a whole within a given city or possibly within a state. It does not preclude activity measurements, but it does direct attention toward areas of priority concern and does provide a semiaggregate view.

In Chapter 6, this method is tested on four functions: education, welfare, police, and fire. These functions were chosen for two reasons. First, together they constitute a large proportion of local government expenditure. Second, output in these four functions is especially difficult to estimate. New York State was used as the test area. Education and welfare were analyzed for the entire state, for New York City, and for the state without New York City. Police and fire were analyzed for the six major New York cities, for New York City, and for the five remaining upstate cities. A case study is also undertaken for one county, analyzing the same four functions.

Conclusion

The overall goal of this study is to provide a means for answering some of those uncomfortable questions asked by the taxpayer about the performance of his local government. The method developed in this work provides such a technique. The results indicate disappointingly low rates of productivity growth for the local government functions examined. If the results are as reliable as they appear to be, a great deal of effort must be directed toward improving local government productivity in the next decade. Chapter 7 makes some recommendations for the direction that this effort should take. It also identifies areas for future research in local government productivity measurement.

Adam Smith once wrote about the "labour of some of the most respectable orders in the society," as being

like that of menial servants, unproductive of any value, and does not fix or realize itself in any permanent subject, or vendible commodity, which endures after that labour is past, and for which an equal quantity of labour could afterwards be procured.[6]

The public servant is "maintained by a part of the annual produce of the industry of other people." His service, no matter "how honourable, how useful, or how necessary" remains like the declamation of the actor, the harangue of the orator, or the tune of the musician, the work of all of them perishes in the very instant of its production.[7]

In the rich language of the eighteenth century, Smith has portrayed the contemporary dilemma of measuring public service. Although Smith said that public service is "unproductive of any value," in reality the public servant is directly engaged in changing social states, in working toward improving the general well-being of the citizenry. It is this change in social states that the citizen perceives as government output. So far it seems impossible to measure changes in social states, but those activities leading to such changes are measurable. This technique developed here provides one method for doing so.

2   Productivity

The purpose of the present chapter is to define productivity in some detail to provide a general review of the methods developed to measure changes in productivity in the private sector. A comprehensive review of private sector productivity measurement is not attempted here; such a review would require a separate volume. Rather, the aim of this chapter is to identify the major theoretical and empirical problems that are encountered in measuring changes in private sector productivity. Although productivity measurement in the private sector is mature and sophisticated when compared to the infant state of the art in the public sector, a number of problems still remain unsolved. Certainly there is no agreement on "a productivity measure." Recognizing these problems is a necessary first step toward realizing the limitations surrounding public sector productivity measurement.

A major portion of this chapter is devoted to an explanation of total factor productivity measurement. The method used in this volume to measure public sector productivity is similar to this method as employed in the private sector.

General Background

Although simple in conception, productivity often becomes misinterpreted and hence ambiguous. In general, *productivity* is a measure of the efficiency with which physical inputs—land, labor, and/or capital—are converted into physical outputs—goods and services. It is a comparison, usually expressed as a ratio, of units of physical output with one or more of the inputs associated with that output. Most physical outputs are not homogeneous and therefore must be converted into homogeneous units before they can be added together. It is meaningless to attempt to add 100 tons of a specified quality of steel to 100 yards of a given quality of cotton cloth. To overcome this problem, units of output are normally multiplied by their constant dollar or real price per unit and expressed as real dollars of output. Weighting in this manner converts heterogeneous into homogeneous output units and expresses those units according to their relative importance in terms of the opportunity cost of each type of output.

Inputs may or may not be weighted by price depending on the particular productivity ratio being used.[1] This ratio indicates the number of units of real output that can be obtained from a given number of units of input. Since the ratio has little meaning by itself, it is usually compared with a corresponding ratio for another time or another place. Such a comparison can then be expressed as an index of productivity. For example, if in 1950 three units of labor produced three dollars of goods and services, while in 1960 those same three units of labor produced six dollars of goods and services in constant prices, productivity has increased by 100 percent. Such an increase over time means that resources are being used more efficiently and that the firm, the industry, or the economy is more productive in 1960 than it was in 1950. As is the case with most other economic concepts, productivity can be measured in terms of averages—average output to average input, or in marginals—the change in output to the change in input.

So far the concept itself seems straightforward enough. Yet the amount of ambiguity and misinterpretation surrounding productivity can to some extent be gauged by the wealth of articles written on "the meaning and measurement of productivity" in recent years. During the last thirteen years, one of the experts in the field, Solomon Fabricant, has felt it necessary to write three major works aimed at correcting the misconceptions surrounding the concept of productivity.[2] Surely some of these misconceptions are the result of catchy definitions popularized by the press. The rather crude phrase "more bang for the buck" is illustrative. Organized labor's perpetual bargaining argument, which equates increased productivity with the increased effort of union members, also confuses the concept. The first definition implies that it is possible for the taxpayer to receive more services for the same tax dollar if only government bureaucrats would work harder or government management would improve. In a sense the implication is that the taxpayer is being cheated by the lazy public servant and the inefficient public manager. This definition reinforces the popularly held American myth that government is inherently inefficient.

On the other hand, labor's use of the term *productivity* implies that unless the worker gets his raise, he is being cheated out of the fruits of his increased work effort and that the worker's effort is being exploited to benefit the capitalist. Both of these definitions relate productivity to the Protestant work ethic. They both specifically tie increased productivity to harder physical work. Such definitions make it as difficult to be against increased productivity as it was to be against economic growth in the late 1950s. The primary result of this popularization process has been to confuse the concept of productivity in the mind of the public.

Two much more fundamental problems are probably of greater importance in explaining the ambiguities surrounding the concept of productivity. The first is the lack of concern in the literature for what productivity is not. Popular definitions of productivity are often so inclusive that they really do not qualify as definitions. The technical literature does little to correct this. Second, the large array of different productivity measures, and hence interpretations, adds to the confusion. "Which productivity?" is often a valid question. An understanding of any specific productivity study requires that the particular method used be *specified* and that its interpretation, including its limitations, be made explicit.

What Productivity Is Not

The production process may be measured in a variety of ways. Productivity measurement is simply one possibility. Unfortunately, discussions of productivity often take place in a vacuum, neglecting the milieu of which productivity measurement is only a part. As a result of this neglect, there is little discussion of either the relationship between productivity and other measures of the production process or of the limitations on the implications which may be drawn from productivity measurement. Perhaps a closer examination of the production process itself will help to identify some of the more important measurement possibilities, the relationships among these different measures, and the types of inferences which may be drawn from each.

In his discussion of public sector outputs, Werner Z. Hirsch describes the production process as follows:

We can visualize the production process in the following manner: Various input factors enter a pipeline in which production converts them into outputs. Since the process takes time, we usually are well advised to assign the production process a time dimension; output is thus measured in the number of units of basic output of specified quality characteristics per unit of time. Output can be produced at a steady or varying rate, which can affect the cost of production as well as the value of the output.[3]

These outputs in turn are expected to generate certain consequences (alternatively called effects, results, or achievements) which either directly or indirectly affect the citizen-taxpayer. The consequences are both positive and negative, wanted and unwanted. Expected consequences are either proxies for, or themselves the ultimate pre-established goals of, the particular public service. Thus, in most cases the consequences rather than the actual outputs are of primary interest to the citizen. A complicating factor is that these consequences are not necessarily the result of one given program output. Rather they are the results of any number of outputs as well as any number of environmental factors which impact on that particular program area.

Police service is a significant example of this process. The goal of a particular police program may be to reduce crime in a given area by 10 percent. To reach this goal, additional men and patrol cars are assigned to the area. The additional men and cars are the inputs in the production process. The activity performed is that these men and cars now patrol the blocks of the area more frequently. The output is the additional number of blocks patrolled in a given period of time.

One possible consequence of this output is that crime falls by 5 percent in the area. The program is halfway to its specified goal. At the same time, crime in another part of the city increases by 10 percent. This increase may be a negative consequence of the same program and must also be included in any evaluation of this particular production process.

Two general categories of measures may be applied to this process: efficiency measures and effectiveness measures. *Efficiency measures* are concerned with the manner in which resources are combined into final products. They do not evaluate the appropriateness of those products. Rather, they take the output as given and inquire only about how that output is provided. In contrast, *effectiveness measures* evaluate the consequences of the product or output.

Although work, cost, and productivity all fall within the efficiency category, each measures different aspects of the production process. Productivity measures refer to the relationship between the results of work activities, the finished product, or the output, and its related inputs. They are measures of the results of work activity, not the activity itself. Work measures, however, examine the work activity itself rather than its results and are usually measured in terms of activity per unit of time. More specifically, *work measures* may be defined as "the conversion of a quantitative statement of the manpower to produce that work load."[4] The measure can then be compared to some engineering or historic standard for that activity, and the conclusion that can be drawn is that the activity is being performed more or less efficiently than the standard. This measure addresses the question of more or less but does not address the question of why the particular activity is performed more or less efficiently.

Of course, there is a relationship between work measures and productivity, but one is not necessarily a simple, direct multiple of the other. Nor can such a direct relationship be inferred simply by knowing the changes in either the work or the productivity measure.

For example, assume that the activity to be analyzed is that of a laborer working on an automobile assembly line. A work measure would analyze the activity of attaching hub-caps, to determine the number of hub-caps installed in a given period of time. If as a result of running rather than walking around the car, our laborer installed more hub-caps per hour, work would have increased. Such an increase may or may not result in increased productivity. The number of hub-caps installed per hour may increase, but the number of finished cars may remain the same. In this case, work has increased while productivity has remained constant.

Again as an example, assume that one is examining the work of a secretary typing letters. A work measure might be the number of letters of a given length and quality typed per hour. An increase in the number of letters typed per hour would only result in an increase in productivity if the additional letters increased the final product—in this case, increased communication.

Admittedly, such examples are extreme, but the point is significant. Work measures are measures of intermediate activity. Productivity measures are concerned with the linkage between final products and inputs. There is a relationship between the two, but contrary to popular wisdom, productivity is not a synonym for harder physical work.

Cost measures in general are expressed as current dollars of inputs per physical or constant dollar units of outputs, whereas productivity measures take the form of physical or constant dollar units of output per physical or constant dollars per unit of input. Both cost and productivity measures have a major advantage over work measures in that both are based upon a general theory of production. From this theory, production functions relating outputs and inputs may be hypothesized. The parameters of the functions may be estimated and tested against the hypothesized relationships. On a superficial level, both cost and productivity measures address the question of more or less. On a more sophisticated level, because of their theoretical basis, both of these measures can be used to address the more important question of why. The reasons for a change in costs or a shift in the production function can be meaningfully discussed. Inferences regarding the workings of the economy can be made and tested.[5] These questions are much more important than the simple question of how much, and in this sense, these two measures are much more powerful than the simple work measures. Emphasizing the importance of this theoretical base, Carl Christ has said:

I feel that shifts of production functions are what productivity indexes are really about, and that in trying to measure productivity, we will be ahead if we remember that production functions are in the theoretical background of what we are doing.[6]

Cost and productivity measures are often related to each other, but they are not identical. An increase in productivity may be reflected in a cost reduction, but a cost reduction is not always the result of an increase in productivity. Thus these two measures are not synonymous, and they should be maintained as distinct indicators of the production process.

Effectiveness measures, on the other hand, attempt to estimate the consequences of a particular program or output. For the private sector, the distinction between efficiency and effectiveness does not constitute a major problem. The goal of the firm is to make profit. To successfully accomplish this goal, the firm must produce those goods or services demanded by the consumer, thus fulfilling the effectiveness criterion. The firm must also produce at a low enough cost so as to remain competitive, thus fulfilling the efficiency criterion.

However, in the public sector the distinction between efficiency and effectiveness is crucial. Suppose, for example, that the goal of a particular governmental program is to reduce the damage done by fires in a given area. One of the activities employed to accomplish this goal may be to install additional fire hydrants in the area. A productivity measure may indicate that the hydrants are being installed very efficiently, but such a measure does not indicate whether or not the additional hydrants have an impact on fire damage. Productivity measures do not address the question of effectiveness. As was pointed out at the Wingspread Symposium in Wisconsin, when dealing with questions of productivity in the public sector,

the government would [will] have to sharpen its essential goals and priorities if greater productivity was [is] to yield meaningful progress. We must, it was urged, keep asking: Efficiency for what? Efficiency for whom?[7]

These are the kinds of questions effectiveness measures attempt to answer.

With the use of planning-programming-budgeting systems, effectiveness measures have become increasingly popular as means of evaluating particular programs. In general, these measures pass over the production process and instead examine the consequences of a program. The measures take three basic forms. They may be expressed as relationships between inputs and consequences, i.e., pupils per teacher and test scores; outputs and consequences, i.e., hours of geography classes and test scores; or consequences and goals, i.e., achieved test scores to wanted test scores. Both the lack of a general theory from which hypotheses can be drawn and tested, and the inability to identify and separate the effects of one particular program from a host of other environmental factors have greatly weakened the evaluation potential of the first two measures. For example, in education there is no good learning theory specifying the expected relationships between pupils per teacher and test scores or between number of hours of geography and the resulting knowledge of geography. Nor has an adequate method been developed for isolating the effects of the number of pupils per teacher on test scores while at the same time holding constant all other factors that may influence scores.

The third measure, the relationship of consequences to goals, is again a "more or less" measure. It indicates how well the program is doing in terms of the previously specified goals, but it does not explain why the program is doing well or poorly.[8]

Some authors contend that efficiency and effectiveness measures can be reconciled with cost effectiveness analysis. These authors may be correct, but as yet no such reconciliation has been successfully accomplished.[9]

The habit of much recent public sector analysis has been to skip entirely the efficiency measures and move directly to measures of effectiveness. Effectiveness measures are important, but not at the expense of cost and productivity measures. Economists have learned a great deal about the private sector by examining the direct outputs of that sector, the cost, and the underlying production functions upon which those outputs are based. The challenge is to develop similar knowledge about the workings of the public sector.

Types of Productivity Measures

The second major reason for the ambiguity surrounding the concept of productivity is the variety of possible measures. These range all the way from direct engineering measures of physical output per unit that may be used on the factory floor, to very indirect measures such as the ratio of price per unit of output to the hourly wage rate of the average worker.[10] Although all of these ratios are measures of productivity, they have different implications. Each is valid if interpreted correctly. This variety coupled with the problems involved in actually measuring outputs and inputs (discussed later in this chapter) can easily lead to misinterpreted results and general public confusion.

In general, productivity measures can be placed in two broad categories: measures that relate output to one input factor (labor, tangible capital, energy, etc.), and measures that relate output to some combination of inputs (normally labor and tangible capital) using some type of weighting to aggregate the combined inputs. Within the first category, the most frequently used measure is output per unit of labor input, referred to as *labor productivity*. Within the second category, *total factor productivity*, output per unit of combined labor and capital, is the most widely used measure.

Labor Productivity

The most important single-factor measure of productivity is labor productivity. Even within this single category, a wealth of possible measures are available. First, labor productivity may be measured for different levels of the economy, ranging from aggregate labor productivity for the economy as a whole to measures of labor productivity for an industry, a firm, or an individual plant. Second, there are a number of ways to count both the output and the labor input. Even at the plant level, products are often not homogeneous and thus require some type of weighting system for meaningful aggregating. Although the weights may be in terms of any unit common to all categories of output—for example, man-hours required per unit of output—the most common weighting procedure is to weight the output by constant money value or constant price. All measures of aggregate productivity use some variant of real gross national product as the measure of output.

Labor inputs may also be counted in a number of ways. Three of the more typical productivity ratios are: (1) output per person employed where the assumption is that persons employed are homogeneous; (2) output per labor-hour where the assumption is that each labor hour constitutes a homogeneous unit; or (3) output per weighted labor-hour where the weights adjust for differences in the quality of the labor input. For example, units of labor may be weighted by average hourly earnings, on the assumption that differences in average earnings reflect differences in labor quality. Output per man-hour is the most frequently used denominator in measures of labor productivity.

At first glance, differences in the way inputs are counted may appear trivial. But when one stops to consider the ramifications, the choice of unit for the denominator becomes quite important. If persons employed is used as the unit of labor input, an increase in either the hours of work (assuming no decreasing returns) or in the quality of labor will appear as an increase in productivity when technically both of these changes should be counted as an increase in labor input. Under the second method, an increase in the hours worked will appear as an increase in inputs, whereas an increase in the quality of labor will show up as an increase in productivity. Under the third method, both an increase in hours worked and an increase in the quality of labor will be counted as an increase in inputs. When comparing productivity measures, units are crucial in determining results.

The most familiar measure of private sector labor productivity at the national level is the index of output per man hour, prepared and published quarterly by the Bureau of Labor Statistics. For this index, *output* is defined as real gross national product originating in the private sector. Labor-hours of employment in the private sector are used as the input measure. Estimates of labor-hours are derived primarily from monthly samples of business firms' payroll records. Estimates of self-employed workers, domestics, and unpaid family workers are derived from sample monthly household surveys. These estimates are based upon hours paid rather than hours actually worked. They include all sick leave, paid vacation and holiday time, and any other hours paid but not actually worked, as well as those hours actually worked.

In addition to the BLS estimates, John W. Kendrick has developed estimates of aggregate labor productivity for the United States.[11] The major difference between Kendrick's estimates and those of BLS is that Kendrick weights the man-hours of labor input in each industry by the average hourly earnings of that industry. The purpose of this procedure is to correct for differences in the quality of man-hours. The assumption underlying this method is that average hourly wage differentials among industries reflect the differences in labor quality among those industries. In his discussion of this weighting procedure, Kendrick states that the different wage rates represent "differences in education, skill, experience, etc. accounting for interindustry differentials in labor quality."[12] He goes on to argue that

since average hourly earnings differ among occupations, roughly reflecting different contributions to product and thus different 'quantities' of labor service, man-hours should be estimated and weighted separately for each occupation. But estimates of employment and hours are generally available over time only on an industry basis; so industry average hourly compensation estimates are used as weights. The aggregate of industry real labor input so computed will approximate the results obtained by weighting man-hours worked by occupational structures if the various industries are relatively stable.[13]

A major difficulty with this method is that relative wage rates reflect a number of factors other than differences in labor quality. For example, differences in the degree of unionization among industries and geographic differences both in terms of different areas of the country and in terms of urban versus rural affect relative pay differentials. A second difficulty is that this method of adjusting for labor quality does not accurately reflect intraindustry changes in the quality of labor because it does not adequately account for occupational changes within an industry.[a] Because of the latter difficulty, weighting in this manner probably underestimates the change in the quality of labor input over time.

As one would expect, these two methods yield different estimates of increases in labor productivity. From 1889 to 1969, output per man-hour for the private economy increased at an average annual rate of 2.4 percent, whereas output per weighted man-hour grew at an average annual rate of only 2.0 percent.[14] This difference is due primarily to the fact that in the latter measure changes in labor quality as reflected by relative wage rates are counted as increases in labor input, whereas in the former method they are not.

The Bureau of Labor Statistics also provides productivity indexes for selected industries. Table 2-1 shows estimates of output per man-hour for 1947-70 and 1957-70 for thirty-eight selected industries. The most interesting aspect of this table is the wide variation in the estimates of output per man-hour. From 1947 to 1970, the average rate of change of output per man-hour for all employees ranged from 1.4 percent in cigarettes, chewing and smoking tobacco, and footwear to 7.8 percent in petroleum pipelines. From 1957 to 1970, the range was even more dramatic, from 0.4 percent in footwear to 10.0 percent for petroleum pipelines. Studies of changes in public sector productivity find similar variations in productivity increases among governmental agencies (see Chapter 4).

A number of single-industry studies of labor productivity also exist. Most of these use an approach similar to the engineering method mentioned earlier and are of particular interest when studied in conjunction with a detailed examination of that particular industry.[15]

Although labor productivity indexes require less information in their construction than do total factor productivity indexes, the former's interpretation requires more care and consideration than the latter. Increases in labor

---

[a]Suppose, for example, a particular industry employed four unskilled union workers at $2.00 per hour. The average wage rate for that industry is $2.00. Now suppose the composition of employment changes within that industry such that it now employs two Ph.D.'s at $3.00 per hour and two unskilled nonunion workers at $1.00 per hour. The average wage rate is still $2.00, but the quality of labor employed may have improved.

Table 2-1
Average Annual Rates of Change in Output per Man-Hour, 1947-70 and 1957-70

Industry Title	Output per Man-Hour: Average Annual Rate of Change (Percentage)[a]					
	1947-70			1957-70		
	All Employees	Production Workers	Nonproduction Workers[b]	All Employees	Production Workers	Nonproduction Workers[b]
Mining						
Iron Mining, Crude Ore	c	5.3	c	c	6.1	c
Iron Mining, Usable Ore	c	2.2	c	c	3.2	c
Copper Mining, Crude Ore	c	4.7	c	c	4.4	c
Copper Mining, Recoverable Metal	c	3.0	c	c	2.6	c
Coal Mining	c	5.9	c	c	5.1	c
Bituminous Coal and Lignite Mining	c	6.0	c	c	5.3	c
Manufacturing						
Canning and Preserving	3.5[d]	3.7[d]	(2.0)[d]	3.0[e]	2.9[e]	(4.0)[e]
Flour and Other Grain Mill Products	4.5	4.7	(3.8)	5.1	5.0	(5.2)
Sugar	4.4	4.6	(3.2)	4.5	4.6	(4.0)
Candy and Other Confectionery Products	3.3	3.2	(3.5)	3.0	2.7	(4.4)
Malt Liquors	4.8	4.9	(4.6)	6.2	6.1	(6.5)
Bottled and Canned Soft Drinks	c	c	c	4.3[f]	4.5[f]	(4.1)[f]
Tobacco Products—Total	3.4	3.6	(1.0)	3.0	3.3	(0.5)
Cigarettes, Chewing and Smoking Tobacco	1.4	1.6	(−0.1)	1.6	1.9	(−0.7)
Cigars	6.1	6.3	(3.3)	5.5	5.7	(3.1)
Hosiery	5.2	5.3	(4.1)	6.3	6.5	(5.0)
Paper, Paperboard and Pulp Mills	3.8	4.1	(1.7)	4.2	4.4	(3.0)
Corrugated and Solid Fiber Boxes	c	c	c	3.2[f]	3.4[f]	(2.7)[f]
Man-Made Fibers	c	c	c	4.7	4.6	(4.8)
Petroleum Refining	5.8	6.3	(4.3)	6.2	6.6	(5.1)

Tires and Inner Tubes	4.1	4.4	(3.1)	4.6	4.7	(4.2)
Footwear	1.4	1.4	(1.2)	0.4	0.4	(0.8)
Glass Containers	1.7	1.7	(0.9)	2.5	2.6	(1.9)
Cement, Hydraulic	4.6	5.0	(2.2)	4.6	5.1	(2.1)
Concrete Products	3.4g	3.8g	(1.6)g	3.7h	3.7h	(3.2)h
Steel	1.7	2.1	(−0.4)	2.2	2.3	(2.0)
Gray Iron Foundries	2.2i	2.2i	(1.7)i	2.4	2.3	(3.0)
Primary Copper, Lead, and Zinc	2.3g	2.5g	(1.0)g	2.2h	2.1h	(2.7)h
Primary Aluminum	4.7	4.9	(3.7)	3.8	3.7	(4.5)
Aluminum Rolling and Drawing	c	c	c	5.2f	5.2f	(5.0)f
Major Household Appliances	c	c	c	5.8f	5.3f	(7.7)f
Radio and Television Receiving Sets	c	c	c	6.0f	5.7f	(7.2)f
Motor Vehicles and Equipment	c	c	c	3.6	3.6	(3.8)
Other						
Railroads, Revenue Traffic	5.2	5.5	2.9	6.0	6.1	4.9
Railroads, Car-Miles	4.1	4.3	1.7	3.7	3.8	2.6
Air Transportation	7.8j	c	c	7.9j	c	c
Petroleum Pipelines	c	c	c	10.0k	10.6k	c
Gas and Electric Utilities	7.0	7.5l	c	6.4	6.8l	c

aBased on the linear least-squares trends of the logarithms of the index numbers.

bRates of change for nonproduction workers (in parentheses) are subject to a wider margin of error than other rates shown.

cNot available.

dAverage annual rate of change is for 1947-68.

eAverage annual rate of change is for 1957-68.

fAverage annual rate of change is for 1958-70.

gAverage annual rate of change is for 1947-69.

hAverage annual rate of change is for 1957-69.

iAverage annual rate of change is for 1954-70.

jOutput per employee.

kAverage annual rate of change is for 1958-69.

lNonsupervisory personnel.

Source: U.S. Department of Labor, Bureau of Labor Statistics, *Indexes of Output per Man-Hour Selected Industries 1939 and 1947-70*, Bulletin 1692 (Washington, D.C.: U.S. Government Printing Office, 1971), p. 7.

productivity as measured by increases in output per man-hour are not solely (or even primarily) the result of improvements in labor efficiency. To attribute such increases entirely to a harder-working labor force, as is often done, is simply wrong. Changes in all single-factor productivity indexes reflect the joint effects of a variety of factors. For example, such a change may merely reflect the substitution of capital for labor inputs. Some of the more important reasons for increases in efficiency are: advances in knowledge, advances in technology and innovations, improvements in management and organization, wider markets resulting in increased specialization and economies of scale, and changes in the mobility of the factors of production. An increase in a labor productivity index may also reflect alterations in the quality of labor resulting from changes in education, age, sex, and so forth, of the labor force. As Fabricant has so succinctly put it:

In short, a change in output per man-hour may be viewed . . . as reflecting the combined effect of change in three things: 1) efficiency as measured by output per unit of labor and capital input; 2) the relative supply of tangible capital as measured by labor and capital input per unit of labor input; and 3) average labor quality as measured by labor input per man-hour.[16]

Partial or single-factor measures of productivity have one grave flaw—they are not discriminating. They do not allow separate estimates of those factors contributing to productivity changes. They therefore must be interpreted with care and the single factor—whether it be labor, capital, energy, or what have you—must not be held solely responsible for changes in the indexes.

Total Factor Productivity

A relatively recent entry into the field of productivity indexes is the so-called total factor productivity index. This index compares changes in output to changes in a weighted sum of labor and capital inputs. To combine labor and capital into an index of inputs, each is weighted by its relative contribution to total inputs. Each factor's relative share of total output is used to estimate this relative contribution. For example, let Y' be an index of total output, L' and K' be indexes of labor and tangible capital inputs, a be labor's relative share of total output and b be tangible capital's relative share of total output, such that $a + b = 1$. Then $aL' + bK'$ is a weighted arithmetic index of labor and capital inputs and $Y' + (aL' + bK')$ is an index of output per unit of labor and capital input, or as it is more commonly called, an index of total factor productivity.[17]

This index measures the efficiency with which labor and capital inputs are converted into outputs. It separates changes in output which result from either increased inputs or input factor substitution from those changes in output which result from greater efficiency. It is a measure of all those forces, i.e., technological progress, and so forth, which contribute to the growth of output, other than capital accumulation or labor force growth. If one's purpose is to measure changes in the productivity of resources as a whole, the total factor productivity index is the proper index to use.

To date this method has been used primarily to identify the sources of economic growth. When used in this context, it is referred to as the residual approach to economic growth. It is based on the assumption of an aggregate production function, and the assumption that there exists a simple, stable relationship between total output and the quantity of total inputs employed in the production of that output. Primarily because of its simplicity, most of the studies in this area have employed a Cobb-Douglas type of function in which

$$Y_t = A_t L_t^a K_t^b .$$

In this case, Y is output in year t; A_t is a measure of total factor productivity, and a and b are the elasticities of output with respect to labor and capital. The output elasticity is the proportional change in output resulting from a given change in one of the inputs; it estimates the relative contributions of labor and tangible capital to total output. In this function, a plus b are normally taken to equal 1 and are constant. Under a fairly rigid set of assumptions, including perfect competition, these coefficients (or weights) may be estimated by the relative factor shares of total output, i.e., that fraction of total value accruing to labor and tangible capital in the base year.[b]

[b]The marginal product of an input is the increase in total output attributable to the addition of one unit of the input to the production process. If the factors are assumed to be paid according to their marginal product, which would be the case when the market is perfectly competitive, then the relative share going to the input is equal to its marginal product and therefore its relative contribution to output. The result is that the factor shares will exactly exhaust the total output. The relative share going to labor and capital can then be used as good approximations of their elasticities. If the economy is in equilibrium, average shares and marginal shares will be equal, thus average shares may be used as estimates of elasticity. There are some other important properties of this function which need to be remembered when it is used in this way. Requiring a plus b to equal 1 means that the function is linearly homogeneous implying constant returns to scale. In this function, the elasticity of substitution between labor and capital is exactly unity. Finally, requiring a and b to remain constant implies neutral technological progress. Shifts in the production function do not change relative marginal products. For additional information on this function, see C.E. Ferguson, *Microeconomic Theory* (Homewood, Ill.: Richard D. Irwin, 1969), pp. 381-89. In estimating the parameters of this function, A may be written as $(1 + r)^t$ where r measures the average annual shift in the production function, interpreted as the rate of technological change and t is measured in years. For more on this point, see Solomon Fabricant, "Productivity," *International Encyclopedia of Social Science*, Vol. 12, David L. Stills, ed. (New York: Macmillan Company and the Free Press, 1968), p. 526.

It should be pointed out that there is a great deal of uneasiness in the economics profession at the moment about private-sector production functions, particularly when these are measured by relative shares. Using relative shares in this way is justified by neoclassical distribution theory. This theory is one of a number of distributive share theories, none of which are completely satisfactory. For an excellent discussion of this point, see Jan Pen, *Income Distribution* (New York: Praeger Publishers, 1971), pp. 158-233, and G.C. Harcourt, *Some Cambridge Controversies in the Theory of Capital* (Cambridge: Cambridge University Press, 1972).

The second step in this process is to develop indexes for output (Y'), labor (L'), and tangible capital (K'), which estimate changes in the quantity of output and labor and tangible capital inputs. The labor input index is often adjusted for changes in the quality of labor. Now $Y' = A'L'^{a}K'^{b}$. Using these indexes, it is possible to estimate A' where A' is the residual or the increase in total output which cannot be explained by the combined increases in labor and tangible capital inputs. A' has alternatively been interpreted as a measure of an increase in knowledge, an increase in total factor productivity (or efficiency), or by some of the more cynical writers, as a measure of our ignorance.[c]

Using this method, a number of authors have estimated the importance of total factor productivity in explaining economic growth.[18] The results of these studies vary. For example, Denison estimates that for the period 1909-57, 77 percent of the growth of total real income was a result of the growth of inputs while the remaining 23 percent was the result of the growth of output per unit of input.[19] D.W. Jorgenson and Z. Griliches estimated that for the period

---

[c]A simple example based on the work of Edward Denison may be helpful. Denison begins with the basic Cobb-Douglas function, $Y = AL^{a}K^{b}$. Taking the logarithm and differentiating, the function may be written as $DY/Y = DA/A + a (DL/L) + b (DK/K)$ where DY/Y is the relative ratio of growth of output, DL/L and DK/K are the relative rates of growth of labor and capital respectively. The terms a and b are the elasticities of labor and capital and are measured by the relative factor shares of labor and capital. Over the period 1929-57, Denison estimates that labor contributed about 73 percent of total input while capital contributed 27 percent. Over the same period, output grew at an actual annual rate of 2.93 percent. The quantity of labor input adjusted for changes in hours increased at an average annual rate of 1.08 percent and therefore contributed 0.79 percentage points (0.73 X 1.08) per year to the growth of output. Thus 27 percent of the growth of output (0.79/2.93) can be attributed to growth in the quantity of labor. Denison then adjusted his quantity of labor index for changes in the quality of labor, specifically for changes in education, age-sex composition, and qualifications of women. Using changes in the quality of education as an example of this adjustment method, Denison estimated that the quality of labor increased at an average annual rate of 0.93 percent and thus contributed 0.68 percentage points (0.93 X 0.73) to the growth of output. Increases in education thus accounted for 23 percent (0.68/2.93) of the growth of real output. After these adjustments, Denison estimates that for the period 1929-57, increases in labor input adjusted for changes in the quality of labor contributed 1.66 percentage points to the growth of output while capital contributed 0.45 percentage points. Thus increases in total inputs accounted for 2.11 percentage points of growth (1.66 + 0.45) while increases in output per unit of input or A accounted for the remaining 0.82 percentage points (2.93 − 2.11). Edward F. Denison, *The Sources of Economic Growth in the United States and the Alternatives Before Us,* Supplementary Paper no. 13 (New York: Committee for Economic Development, 1962).

It should be noted that there are other methods for estimating the contribution of total factor productivity to growth. Using multiple regression techniques, the coefficients of labor and capital may be estimated rather than assuming they are approximated by relative factor shares. The results of such a process are to increase the coefficient of capital and therefore reduce the contribution of output per unit of total inputs. If the constraint of constant returns to scale is dropped, the a and b are estimated, the result is that much more of the rate of growth can be explained by increasing returns to scale. Although both of these methods are possible and both reduce the residual, there is some question as to whether or not either of these methods provide any greater economic insights into the sources of economic growth. Richard R. Nelson, "Aggregate Production Functions and Medium-Range Growth Projections," *American Economic Review* 54 (September 1964): 579-580.

1945-65 increases in inputs explain 96.7 percent of the growth of total output, while total factor productivity explains only the remaining 3.3 percent.[20] Although a part of the difference in the estimated importance of total factor productivity to economic growth is a result of the differences in the time periods covered, more important are the differences in what is actually measured and how these measurements are adjusted for changes in quality. On the whole, all of these studies find that shifts in the production function and changes in total factor productivity are important in explaining economic growth.

Although the total factor productivity approach to measuring changes in efficiency has received some severe criticism,[21] it does possess a number of important advantages. The approach is comprehensive in nature. The factors can be quantified and therefore measured. By forcing the analyst to specify the production function, his assumptions concerning the shape of the relationship between output and inputs must be explicitly stated. Although the approach is at the highest level of aggregation, it does indicate the direction in which the economy is moving, and it does provide estimates of the relative magnitudes of the factors involved in that movement. As Joan Robinson has said,

A highly aggregated model is useful only for a first sketch of the analysis of reality, but it is much easier to fill in the details in the outline drawn by a simple model than it is to build up an outline by amassing detail.[22]

Given the different methods available for measuring productivity and the variety of possible interpretations of each of these methods, the ambiguity and perhaps some of the mystique surrounding this concept is understandable. Analysts in this area could help to reduce the amount of misunderstanding by being more explicit in the interpretation of their results. Rather loose, vague statements concerning results add to an already confused situation. Even after the differences in method have been examined, there is another set of problems which makes for differing results. These are the problems involving the actual measurement of both inputs and outputs and are important enough to deserve some discussion.

Measuring Outputs and Inputs

Even those productivity measures most thoroughly conceived are in practice still only crude approximations of ideal measures. The reasons for this gap between the ideal and the practical center around the lack of necessary statistical information required for the ideal index. Most of the aggregate information that is available has been collected for purposes other than productivity measurement. For example, information used to estimate output usually comes from gross national product accounts. These accounts were developed to estimate the aggregate operation of the economy, not to serve as the ideal numerator of a productivity index. Fitting the available information into the requirements of productivity indexes has created some conceptual problems, many of which are still not solved to anyone's satisfaction. These problems may be classified into two general categories: (1) problems associated with the measurement of output; and (2) problems associated with the measurement of input.

To fit the available measures of aggregate output into the rather stringent parameters prescribed for the numerator of a productivity index requires that some essential decisions be made. The most crucial of these decisions concern the choice of net versus gross output, how the output is to be valued, and which part of total output is to be included. After these decisions have been made, the identification of possible biases inherent in the output measures must be accomplished. All of these decisions are crucial because they influence the inferences that can be drawn from the productivity index; they affect the interpretation and comparability of different indexes.

Outputs

The ideal measure of output for an aggregate productivity index is value added or net output. Theoretically, the goal is to relate the net addition in output to the contributions of the factor inputs. The constant dollar value of production minus the constant dollar value of the labor and capital attributable to that production would constitute such a measure. Unfortunately for productivity measurement, the present United States income and product accounts do not provide very reliable estimates of value added. Net national product comes closest to measuring value added, but the estimates of capital consumption used to derive this measure are unreliable. In the national income and product accounts, capital depreciation is used to estimate capital consumption. Depreciation is an accounting concept and the methods used to calculate it depend upon existing tax laws. Capital consumption, on the other hand, should be an estimate of the actual quantity of capital used up in the production process, unrelated to depreciation for tax purposes. Thus the analyst who attempts to measure aggregate productivity is in a predicament. He has a choice between using as his measure of output either gross national product, which is theoretically incorrect but whose estimate is reasonably reliable, or net national product, which is theoretically correct but whose estimate is unreliable.

One faces a second dilemma when making the choice between gross and net measures of output; that is, the choice of the output estimate should be consistent with the choice of the measures of inputs. In their study, Jorgenson and Griliches use real gross national product on the ground that it is more comparable to the measurement of factor input quantities. "Exclusion of depreciation on capital introduces an entirely arbitrary distinction between labour input and capital input, since the corresponding exclusion of depreciation of the stock of labour services is not carried out."[23] In other words, they believe that it is incorrect to compare a net measure of output with a gross measure of labor input.

In *Why Growth Rates Differ*, Denison takes the opposite approach to measuring output. He uses national income or net national product valued at factor cost on the ground that

insofar as a large output is a proper goal of society and objective of policy, it is net product that measures the degree of success in achieving this goal. Gross product is larger by the value of capital consumption. There is no more reason to wish to maximize capital consumption—the quantity of capital goods used up in production—than there is to maximize the quantity of any intermediate product used up in production, such as, say, the metal used in making television sets. It is the television sets, not the metal or machine tools used up in production, that is the object of the production process.[24]

Denison uses net output on the theoretical ground that there is no reason to include in the output measure the quantity of intermediate goods used up in the production process. He insists that his position introduces no arbitrary distinction between the way labor and capital inputs are counted because, as far as he is concerned, there is no such thing as labor depreciation comparable to capital depreciation. Elaborating on this, Denison says,

I am not aware of a definable labor counterpart to capital depreciation as a component of GNP that there is no advantage in increasing because it is not wanted—feeding, clothing, and housing children surely do not fall into this category—but if there be such, the appropriate remedy would be to change the measures of output and labor earnings.[25]

The choice between net or gross also has implications for the way in which taxes are treated. The treatment of taxes affects relative factor shares and therefore the weights applied to labor and capital inputs. The primary concern here is the short-run incidence of the indirect business tax. How are the returns from this tax to be appropriated between labor and capital inputs? Jorgenson and Griliches allocate the returns from this tax to capital, thus increasing capital's relative share. Denison argues that this treatment is incorrect and results in overweighting capital as compared to labor.[26]

After the decision between gross or net has been made, one must decide which gross or net to use as the measure of output. Three choices are available: (1) total product; (2) domestically produced product; or (3) private domestically produced product. Again the choice of the numerator has implications for the conclusions which may be drawn from the index. The use of total gross or net national product includes the foreign sector, and the resulting productivity index will reflect the gains or losses in foreign trade. This index depends to a degree on changes in productivity in other countries. The usual procedure is to use domestically produced gross or net national product as the numerator in an aggregate productivity index.

The choice between total domestic product and private domestic product introduces the question of whether or not to include the public sector as a part of the aggregate productivity measure. In the GNP accounts, the quantity of output in government is measured by the constant dollar value of its inputs, mainly the wages and salaries of government workers, at factor costs. When the quantity of output is estimated in this way, by the quantity of input, and then related to the changes in inputs, obviously there can be no statistical change in productivity. Assuming that productivity in the public sector has increased, estimating output for a large sector of the economy on the assumption that there is no increase in this sector biases the entire aggregate index downward. Thus most aggregate indexes use only privately produced domestic product as the output numerator.

Finally, these output measures suffer from all of the standard estimating problems surrounding the measurement of GNP. For example, they do not include most nonmarket transactions such as the value of the services of a housewife. They do not include external costs of production, but they do include the value of goods or services produced to correct those external costs. Because of the inadequacies of the price indexes used for deflation, GNP estimates do not provide reliable estimates of changes in the quality of many goods and services. More specifically, a cost index rather than a price index is used for deflation in the construction industry. Such an index does not adequately account for improvements in the utilization of labor or materials. The result is an overstatement of price increases and thus an understatement of changes in efficiency in this industry.[27] Difficulties in quantifying output in the service area result in especially weak GNP output estimates in this sector.

These are just a few of the problems associated with using GNP estimates as measures of output. But these examples are sufficient to indicate the extreme care which must be exercised in such use and in interpreting the results of productivity indexes based upon these estimates.[28]

Inputs

Although there are problems associated with the measurement of both labor and capital individually, when dealing with total factor productivity the overriding issue concerns the classification of changes in factor inputs among labor, capital, and the residual. This issue arises because of the lack of a generally accepted theory which links technological change, factor inputs, and output. How is technological change translated into increased output? Perhaps it is through improvements in the quality of labor. If so, the quantity of labor should be adjusted for such quality changes. Is it translated through improvements in the quality of capital? If so, then the quantity of capital should be adjusted to reflect such changes. Some combination in the quality of both labor and capital may turn technological change into increased output. If so, then how does one adjust labor and capital inputs? Or, should all such increases in output resulting from technological improvements simply be left as part of the unexplained residual?

Some economists, exemplified by Jorgenson and Griliches, believe that if labor and capital inputs are totally adjusted for quality changes, total factor productivity would be very small. Others, such as Denison, feel that even if the inputs are totally adjusted for quality changes, changes in total factor productivity would still be an important source of economic growth. These questions raise the whole issue of exactly what total factor productivity measures. The way different authors classify changes in factor inputs affects the interpretation of what is meant by total factor productivity.

In the literature the controversy rages between those who would adjust the quantity of labor inputs for changes in quality resulting from technological changes and those who would make the necessary adjustments on the capital input. Some writers argue that technological change is translated into additional output via changes in the skills, training, and education of the labor force.[29] Others argue that such technology is embodied in new capital stock, making necessary an adjustment to new capital reflecting its additional productive capacity.[30]

Between these two extremes, there are those writers who stress, as the vehicle of technological change, the interaction both among factor inputs and between these inputs and the residual. Certainly there is both complementarity and substitutability among factor inputs, and these complementary and substitute relations are affected by technological change. Interaction also exists between factor inputs and the residual. For example, a better-educated labor force increases both the quality of labor and the rate of technological understanding, and hence the rate of technological change. As Nelson has argued, "both directly and indirectly, there is complementarity between the rate of growth of total factor productivity resulting from better allocating resources (labor and capital), and the rate of growth of the capital stock. This is not embodiment in the Solow sense, but it has the same effect."[31] Nelson believes that lack of a theory at this level and lack of the recognition of interaction does damage to all quality adjustments and therefore to the entire concept of total factor productivity.

In sum, the aggregative production function may be a useful part of the framework for studying economic growth, but it is a mistake to try to introduce into the production function variables such as average years of education without an explicit theory that shows how that variable should be entered.[32]

Following this logic, attempts to reduce either the factor inputs or the residual to fine components may only be an exercise in futility. It would not increase the understanding of the reasons for increases in productivity.

Lack of a theory incorporating technology into the production function leads to very practical "nuts and bolts" problems involving the proper classification of certain types of inputs. Should certain quantity and quality changes be classified as changes in factor inputs or should they remain as a part of the residual? For example, Jorgenson and Griliches classify capital inputs into sixteen different categories, each with an independent relative weight.[33] Denison argues that such a procedure transfers improvements resulting from the allocation of resources out of the residual and makes them a part of changes in factor inputs, thus distorting the entire concept of productivity.

If the distinction between output growth achieved by an increase in total factor input and output growth achieved by an increase in total factor productivity has any meaning, output gains or losses resulting from the shift of an input from one use to another surely belongs in the productivity series.[34]

A second but related issue concerns the way in which adjustments are made for changes in resource utilization. By their very nature, productivity models are supply models, looking exclusively at supply characteristics and ignoring increases in demand as a possible source of productivity increase. Certainly growth and productivity can be increased by increasing aggregate demand. To stop changes in resource utilization from appearing as productivity increases, adjustments must be made to correct for such changes. Two general methods are used to make this kind of correction. One method is to choose beginning and ending periods of approximately the same level of resource utilization and to study a period of time long enough such that, in the aggregate, the adjustments work themselves out. The second method is to adjust labor and tangible capital for changes in utilization. Denison makes this adjustment by his assumption concerning the effects of a shorter workweek on the quantity of work actually performed. Jorgenson and Griliches supply a method for adjusting for changes in capital utilization. They begin by assuming that all classes of capital are utilized to the same degree. They then assume that the relative use of electric motors is a good proxy for the relative utilization of all capital. Finally, they adjust their capital series by the rate of utilization of electric motors.[35] The result of this adjustment is to increase capital input. The capital utilization adjustment employed by Jorgenson and Griliches accounts for the major part of the difference between their estimates of total factor productivity and those generated by Denison.[36]

Added to these two theoretical problems are the more practical issues encountered in measuring labor and capital inputs.

Labor Inputs. In estimating the quantity of labor, two obstacles are immediately encountered. The first concerns the homogeneity of labor, the second the more practical issue of labor force coverage. The ideal measure of labor input is homogeneous man-hours worked. Given such a measure, one could obtain a reliable estimate of labor input by simply adding up these homogeneous man-hours. Unfortunately, gross man-hours are not homogeneous; there is a wide variation in the quality of these hours. Merely to add gross man-hours implies that the hours of labor of the ditch digger and those of the brain surgeon are identical in quality, that the hours of labor of the high school dropout and those of the Ph.D. provide identical contributions to output. In a few extreme cases, such an implication may of course be correct, but in most instances the quality differences actually constitute differences in the quantity of labor input. The brain surgeon's contribution to total output is usually greater than that of the ditch digger; the contribution of the Ph.D. is usually greater than that of the high school dropout.

Although many estimates of productivity simply ignore this problem, the more sophisticated measures make at least some attempt at correcting for differences in the quality of man-hours. Two general methods for making this correction have been used: Kendrick's average pay differential discussed earlier in this chapter and Denison's method. Denison's method involves weighting man-hours for changes in the length of education, training, and/or age-sex composition of the labor force to adjust for quality changes. The implied assumption is that there is a close relationship between the quality of man-hours and these three factors. The weakness in this method is that the weights used for adjustment are necessarily arbitrary.

The second major issue that must be confronted when attempting to estimate the quantity of labor input concerns the gaps in the coverage of man-hours.[37] The primary source of such information is payroll data on employment. This source can be supplemented by labor force series based on sample household surveys, but those two series are not strictly compatible. Hours for supervisors in nonmanufacturing industries are not available, and most information on man-hours refers to hours paid rather than hours worked. At best only estimates of the actual quantity of labor can be obtained.

Capital Inputs. Although estimating the quantity of labor inputs is difficult, it is probably not as troublesome as measuring capital inputs. Capital inputs should be measured by the flow of capital services. As Mark has pointed out, ideally, "an aggregate of the capital hours used weighted by the rental value of each type of structure and piece of equipment is needed."[38] Unfortunately, such a measure is not available.

Most studies base their measures of capital input on estimates of capital stock, accomplished by simply adjusting the value of existing plant and equipment for new investment and for the retirement of old assets. Capital stock may be estimated in gross or net terms. If gross, the asset is retained at full value until it is retired from use. Capital stock is not a dependable proxy for capital flow, because of the necessity for adjusting for changes in the intensity of use, as noted above. Such estimates do not take into account the probable loss in productive efficiency that occurs as the asset grows older. Some analysts have suggested that the stock should be weighted for the embodiment of new technology on the theory that new capital, because of its improved built-in technology, has a greater productive capacity than that capital which it replaces. Few analysts have actually tried such a procedure because of the difficulties involved in determining the proper weights to use. Does a new machine have twice the productive capacity of the machine it replaces? Or, does it have three times the productive capacity?

Standard capital stock estimates are available and most of the productivity studies draw their measure of capital input from one of these series. The Department of Commerce prepares twelve different capital series annually, all within the framework of the national income accounts.[39] Another popular source is the estimates developed by Goldsmith.[40] These two sources do differ and these differences will affect the results of any given study.

Summary

The purpose of this chapter has been to explore the concept of productivity and in the process to remove some of the popular confusion surrounding its meaning. Productivity is a relatively simple concept, developed within the framework of neoclassical production theory. Unfortunately, changes in productivity may be measured in a variety of ways ranging all the way from partial, single-factor estimates to total-factor estimates. Each measure has its own interpretation; there is really no such thing as "a" productivity measure. In analyzing productivity changes, one must be specific in explaining the measure of productivity he is employing.

Although there are a number of operational and theoretical problems that plague private sector productivity measurements, they still provide useful insights into the workings of the private economy. One would expect studies of public sector productivity to provide similar useful insights. The next chapter will explore some of the problems that must be faced in measuring productivity for the public sector.

3 Public-Sector Output

The difficulties associated with estimating outputs and inputs in the public sector are closely related to the general problems discussed in Chapter 2. The major difference is that for the public sector the complications are carried to the extreme. Even the most basic requirements for a productivity index—independent, reliable estimates of outputs and inputs—are not readily available.

This chapter reviews the difficulties surrounding the estimation of public sector outputs, beginning with an examination of concepts of private service output estimation. The second part of this chapter examines the methods developed for estimating private sector services, some of which are relevant for measuring the quantity of public sector output. These methods are reviewed in the final part of this chapter.

The national income and product accounts, the major source of output information for aggregate productivity indexes, do not provide independent estimates of public sector products. Without independent estimates, the productivity analyst is left with two choices. He may either omit the public sector from his estimates of aggregate productivity, or he may simply assume some rate of productivity increase in the public sector and include the sector at that rate. Given the importance of this sector as a major resource user, the analyst's choice regarding this matter will appreciably affect his estimates of aggregate productivity change.

Significance of the Public Sector

Jerome A. Mark has developed estimates of these effects.[1] Tables 3-1 and 3-2 report his findings. Table 3-1 shows the effects of assuming one rate for the entire public sector. For the period 1950-71, the average annual rate of productivity improvement in the private sector was 3.0 percent. If one assumes a zero percent improvement in the government sector, the implied rate for the total economy becomes 2.5 percent. The average annual rate of productivity increase falls by 0.5 percentage points. If, in contrast, one assumes a public sector productivity rate of 4.0 percent, the implied national rate becomes 3.2 for a gain of 0.2 percentage points.

Table 3-2 estimates the effects of assuming an average annual rate of productivity improvement of 1.9 percent in the federal sector and then varying the assumed rate of increase in the state and local sector. Note that by varying

Table 3-1

Effect on the National Rate of Productivity Growth of Various Assumed Rates of Productivity Growth in the Omitted Government Sector (Percentage)

Average Annual Rate of Productivity Improvement in Private Sector Measures,[a] 1950-71	Assumed Rate of Improvement in Omitted Sectors of Government	Implied National Rate of Total Economy
3.0	0.0	2.5
3.0	1.0	2.7
3.0	2.0	2.8
3.0	3.0	3.0
3.0	4.0	3.2

[a]Includes government enterprises.
Note: The private sector measure excludes 17.1 percent of total man-hours – those worked in the public sector.

Table 3-2

Effect on Total National Productivity Growth of Alternative Rates of State and Local Government Productivity (Percentage)

Private Rate (Less Government Enterprises) 1950-71	Assumed Federal Rate	Assumed State and Local Rate	Implied National Rate
3.1	1.9	0.0	2.7
3.1	1.9	1.0	2.8
3.1	1.9	2.0	2.9
3.1	1.9	3.0	3.0
3.1	1.9	4.0	3.1

Source: Jerome A. Mark, "Progress in Measuring Productivity in Government," *Monthly Labor Review* 95 (December 1972): 5.

the assumed rate of productivity increase in state and local government between 0.0 and 4.0 percent per year, the implied national rate of productivity growth varies between 2.7 and 3.1 percent per year.

Actually, the real bias may be much greater than these simple statistics would indicate. Two factors are essential here. First, if one agrees with the Galbraithian hypothesis of underinvestment in the entire public sector,[2] then by increasing public sector investment, productivity in the private sector will be increased. When the public sector is ignored or when no change is assumed, the aggregate index will pick up the increase in private-sector productivity that results from the increase in public-sector investment, but it will attribute this increase to the wrong source and the implications that are drawn will be incorrect. The bias may also be greater than would be expected because of the externalities involved in the production and consumption of public sector goods and services. For example, the social value of education or law enforcement may be much greater than the costs of providing these services.[a] Thus the analyst is left with the choice of either leaving out a large and growing sector of the economy, or including it, but under very unreliable estimating conditions. In either case, the index will not accurately reflect the entire economy.

The Conceptual Problem

There is general agreement that using inputs to measure outputs is not a viable method for obtaining reliable output estimates. But there is no general agreement as to how to improve the existing estimates, mostly because of the lack of an agreed-upon method for directly estimating public sector product. The inability to measure output directly in the public sector is the major obstacle blocking attempts at estimating changes in government productivity.

This obstacle has both a quantity and a quality dimension. Related to both of these dimensions is the fact that direct prices are not usually charged for public services. Most goods and services provided by the public sector are at least to some extent "public," meaning that quantities of the good or service cannot be divided among consumers. Units may not be purchased individually and the citizen has little direct choice over the quantities of the good he consumes. At the extreme, the case of the pure public good, individual exclusion is impossible and the good must be consumed in equal amounts by all. Of course most of the goods and services provided by the public sector, particularly the local public sector, are not "public" in the above sense of the word. The normal justification for public provision of "nonpublic" goods is the large quantity of externalities surrounding their production or consumption. No practical method for meaningfully pricing these externalities has yet been developed. Private sector provision of such goods and services would result in a misallocation of resources; therefore they are publicly provided. Without direct pricing, it is impossible to estimate output value in the usual way. The total value of output to the consumer, price times quantity, cannot be calculated.

---

[a]This is the first distinction between private and social benefits and costs that has been mentioned. The reason for not discussing this point earlier is that productivity indexes ignore this distinction and deal only in terms of private benefits and costs. This, of course, is due to the difficulty of estimating social benefits and costs. Since the public sector deals in goods and services with large quantities of externalities, when making the decision as to whether or not to include the public sector in the index this distinction must be recognized.

Even without a direct price, estimates of public sector ouput and thus productivity could be based solely on physical quantity. But for most goods and services provided by the public sector, easily definable, physical units of output are not available. Most public sector outputs are in the nature of services and, as is the case with private services, they are produced and consumed in a single operation effectively eliminating a physical unit of output.

For many public services, there is no agreement as to what the unit of output should be. For example, it is quite misleading and even rather meaningless to discuss the number of units of education. What is a unit of education? Is it the number of hours spent in class? Is it the amount of material covered in those hours? Is it the number of contact hours with a teacher holding a certain degree? One can obviously speak in terms of more education versus less education in the sense that the college graduate has had more exposure to educational institutions than the high school dropout. But to speak in terms of how much more, or how many more units, some definition of a unit must be agreed upon. Reaching such an agreement has proved to be an extremely frustrating task.

In those instances where a quantity unit is available and can be agreed upon, to be additive that unit must be made homogeneous with respect to quality. Suppose, for example, that one wants to measure the output of trash collection. The unit of output is the number of tons of trash collected per week. Certainly there is a difference in the quality of the service if the trash is picked up twice rather than once a week, or if it is collected from behind the house rather than from the curb. The problem is, how does one adjust the number of tons of trash collected for these differences in the quality of the pick-up? Again as an example, assume that for education the agreed-upon unit of output is the number of hours devoted to a specific subject. Certainly those hours differ in terms of what is learned. How does one correct for the differences in the quality of each of those hours? How does one make the learning potential of each hour homogeneous? In the private sector, where direct prices are available, real price changes may be used to reflect changes in quality and therefore changes in total value. Yet even here, as the work done on hedonistic price indexes will attest, estimates of quality change are still not particularly reliable.[3] Without a direct price, holding quality constant or making the necessary adjustments to correct for quality changes becomes very complex. Yet without the necessary quality adjustments, estimates of quantity changes can be very misleading.

One method of approaching these obstacles is to use proxies such as test scores, crime rates, or mortality rates as estimates for public service output, in this case for education, police, and health services. respectively. These proxies indicate the consequences of public services. They measure the effects of providing such services rather than the quantity or quality of the services actually being delivered. Using such measures to estimate government output is analogous to using the number of miles traveled by car as a measure of car production in the private sector. The provision of public services has affected the whole character of our society, but attempts to measure the change in that character and define it as public output are not analogous to the way in which private output is defined.

When using proxies in this way, an additional complication which must be faced is that most public services have no single, clear objective function for the proxy to represent. Most public services, as they are normally defined, have a multiplicity of goals or functions, and it is very difficult to objectively establish the relative importance of any one of these goals. Administrators of most public services generally refuse to single out any objective as most important. Rather, when asked about goals, they will identify a list of objectives, all of importance. Any one program has multiple goals.

For example, the objectives of a local school district may include any or all of the following: (1) maximizing the achievement of the average child; (2) maximizing the achievement of the very bright child; (3) maximizing the achievement of the handicapped child; and/or (4) providing job skills to persons previously unskilled or unemployable. As can be seen from this simple list, some of the goals may actually conflict. Such a multiplicity of objectives makes any single-purpose behavioral model, such as those used in the private sector, unworkable in the public sector. To argue that the results of voting identifies a single goal which should be maximized not only ignores Arrow's impossibility theorem,[4] but is inaccurate in behavioral terms. Voters are normally not given a single, clearly defined goal on which to vote. As a result, when voting, voters are not attempting to maximize a single behavioral function; rather they are expressing a multitude of wants with their votes. If proxies are to be used, a number of proxies must be developed for each function, one for each of the goals of that function, and each weighted according to the relative importance of the goal it represents—a very difficult task at best.

Goals change over time, and the proxies representing these goals must also change. Assume that in period 1 the primary goal of one school district was to get every pupil through the eleventh grade. A proxy measuring this goal may be the percentage of pupils actually completing the eleventh grade. Suppose that in time period 2, the goal of that same school district is to have every pupil complete the thirteenth grade. The percentage of pupils completing the eleventh grade can no longer be used to represent the output of the school district. A different output is now being sought. Any method that attempts to estimate public sector output by using proxies to measure the goals of the public sector must be able to incorporate such changes into its estimating procedure.

In some circumstances it may be possible to use proxies as well as the quantity of public sector output. The general procedure is to select as proxies factors which represent changes in the quality of the output. To adjust the change in the quantity of output for changes in quality, the output estimate is multiplied by the percentage change in the quality proxy. When one considers this method of using proxies to estimate changes in quality, two problems become immediately apparent.

The first concerns the choice of quality proxies. Which factors should be chosen as quality indicators? The answer to this question depends upon value judgments as to what the service should actually be. These judgments may be made by the consumer, by the administrator, or by the analyst.[5] There is no reason for the judgment of these three groups to be unanimous. Indeed, there is apt to be disagreement as to whether or not a particular change is an improvement in quality. For example, with computerized procedures, welfare checks may be distributed with much greater speed. Whether or not this increase in speed is an improvement in the quality of the welfare service depends upon what one thinks that service should entail. If the goal is to distribute the checks more efficiently, then computerization of the department is certainly an improvement in the quality of the service. If, on the other hand, one feels that the primary goal is to "get the cheaters off the welfare rolls" then improving the speed with which checks are distributed does not constitute a major quality improvement.

The second problem concerns the types of quantity changes which may qualify as quality proxies. Can changes in the quantity of inputs (i.e., a reduction in the teacher/pupil ratio) be used as a proxy for changes in the quality of outputs? Most studies of public sector output have implicitly answered this question in the affirmative by using such changes as output quality proxies. By adjusting the quantity of output with proxies representing changes in the quantity or quality of both inputs and outputs, one is never sure if he has adequately adjusted for all quality changes or if he has simply double-counted.

Along with these two major problems surrounding quality proxies, there is the entire question of how to weight these different measures. Should all changes in quality be given the same weight or are some more important than others? If some are more important, what is their relative importance? Again without objective measures, the only answers to these questions lie in individual value judgments.

To date, none of these three problems involving the use of proxies to estimate changes in the quality of public sector output have been successfully solved. Most studies of public sector ouput use some type of quality proxies simply because without quality adjustment, estimates of quantity may be worse than meaningless. In the final analysis, how valid these proxies are depends upon the analyst's accuracy of judgment.

Other problems are also encountered in the public sector which make productivity difficult to estimate. One of these is that most public services are vertically integrated. The government both produces and distributes the good or service, and it is impossible to separate production productivity from distribution productivity. If public sector productivity followed the pattern of the private sector, one would expect a different rate of productivity change for production than for distribution, and the rate of productivity growth to be greater for production than for the distribution of the good or service. For policy decisionmaking, it would be very helpful if these two rates could be separated. In practice, such a separation is not possible.

A second obstacle to the measurement of productivity in the public sector is that there are no reliable estimates of capital input for this sector. Capital expenditures are treated as current expenditures in the national income accounts. There are no estimates of depreciation for public sector capital. Capital in the public sector is large and growing, but dependable estimates of its contribution to public output do not exist. Goldsmith has estimated that in constant prices the net stock of tangible assets of states and local governments increased from $16.23 billion in 1900 to $130.74 billion in 1958, while that of the federal government increased from $6.39 billion to $72.13 billion over the same period of time.[6] These are sizable quantities ignored in the public sector in estimating productivity.

Measuring productivity in private sector services confronts many of the same obstacles that must be faced in public sector productivity measurement. Services in both sectors are intangible and difficult to count, but to date measurements of private sector services have been more successful. Because of the similarities, it is worth examining the way productivity has been measured in this area.

Private Sector Service Productivity

Estimating the quantity and quality of service output constitutes the major stumbling block to measuring productivity in the service area. Often, no measurable physical unit of a given quality dimension is available for counting. For example, how does one quantify the repair of TV sets, or more generally, the provision of private health care?

Two general methods of measuring the quantity of services have been developed to overcome this problem. The number of direct outputs, for example, the number of TV sets repaired, the number of hospital operations performed, or the number of meals served in a restaurant, may be counted. This method of estimating service quantities is open to two criticisms. First, such estimates do not take into account differences in the quality of the direct output. The atypical case of a TV set repair which lasts for a few years is certainly of a higher quality than the more typical case in which the life of the repaired set can be counted in weeks. A meal served at Tour D'Argent certainly differs from one served by MacDonald's. Counted aggregates of direct outputs do not take these quality differences into account. One possible solution is to break the direct outputs into finer and finer categories until the categories themselves become so well defined that by definition they correct for quality differences. Besides the obvious problem of an infinite number of possible categories, this solution faces a second general criticism—the direct outputs do not actually represent the desired service output. The result desired by the consumer is often a combination of direct outputs rather than the individual direct output.

In the case of TV set repairs, although the number of tubes replaced may be a valid direct output measure, the desired service output is that the TV set now works. The performance of an operation may be broken down into any number of sets of activities, but the desired output is still that the patient be made well. When viewed from the consumer's perspective, even activities so finely broken down as to be homogeneous in quality yield only rough estimates of the quantity of services provided.

To overcome these obstacles, a second method for estimating the quantity of service output has been suggested—to measure the effects or consequences of the service. In this case, the quantity of TV repair service is measured by the number of working TV's. The quantity of medical service may be measured by changes in the death rate. This method confuses service output and the effects or consequences of the service. These effects are not necessarily a direct result of the service; rather they are a result of both the service and the environment within which the service is provided. To use consequences as estimates of service output requires that one be able to separate those effects which directly result from the service from those effects which result from the environment within which that service is performed—often a difficult, if not impossible, task. A second difficulty is that other private sector products are not measured in terms of their consequences. To be analogous, the output of airplanes, for example, would have to be measured in terms of the number of passenger miles traveled or the number of tons of freight moved. Without analogous measures, it is very hard to compare the quantity of service output with the quantity of output provided by the rest of the private sector.

Thus, although both of these methods have some merit, neither provides an ideal measure of the quantity of service output. As Burkhead and Miner have argued in their evaluation of these two methods,

both views have merit, but economic analysis has stubbornly eschewed measurement of quantities of goods in terms of their consequences because of the considerable advantages in maintenance of the distinction between output and evaluation.[7]

The private service sector has one clear distinction as compared with the public sector. Private sector services are sold in the market and therefore have a market price. Thus total value, theoretically price times quantity, can be estimated. Assuming a competitive market, marginal price equates value to the consumer with cost to the producer.

In his studies of productivity in the service sector, Fuchs provides examples of both the direct output and the object function or consequences methods.[8] The best examples are contained in his three detailed case studies: retail trade, barber and beauty shops, and private medical care. The first two cases use what amounts to a direct output estimate of product. The third also uses the direct output method, but in addition, it presents a detailed discussion of how the object-function method may be applied to medical care.

In estimating retail trade output, input prices and internal efficiency are both specified and taken into account by Fuchs. The object in this case is to measure the quantity of services, including storage, credit, information, and so forth, provided by the retailers. The method used is to measure the real quantity of goods sold by the retailer. Current dollar sales for each type of retail store (where type is defined by the kind of goods sold) are deflated by a price index, weighted by the average gross margin of each store type, and summed by type. The average gross margin is the ratio of total sales minus total cost of all goods sold to total sales. Thus the average gross margin is a ratio of value added to total sales or percentage of value added. Types of stores with larger margins are given heavier weight in the output index on the assumption that larger margins reflect larger quantities of retail services provided per real dollar's worth of goods sold. Underlying this entire approach is the assumption that "the quantity and quality of services supplied by retailers per constant dollar's worth of goods sold remains constant over time within each type of store."[9]

This assumption may be questioned on several grounds. First, it does not adequately recognize variations over time in quantity and quality of services provided by different stores within the same retail store type. A second and perhaps more important criticism is that this method assumes that the size of the margin reflects differences in the quantity of services provided among different store types. Only in a competitive market would this assumption necessarily hold true. Only there would the margin necessarily be a valid measure of value added. Some writers have argued that a reduction in margin may reflect greater efficiency in retailing with no loss in the quantity or quality of services provided. The growth of discount houses is suggested as proof of this, on the argument that such stores offer basically the same services as more conventional stores.

A third problem with this method concerns the size of the transaction. An increase in the size of the transaction may or may not involve a proportional increase in the quantity of services rendered. The present method assumes that there is a proportional increase; but it may be convincingly argued that increases in average dollar size of transactions do not necessarily involve proportional increases in quantity of services. Is more service actually performed by the store when one buys ten shirts in a single transaction than when one buys only one shirt? Those who argue that an increase in dollar size does not involve a proportional increase in service also usually argue in favor of relying on the number of transactions in that it is analogous to the way output is estimated in the rest of the private sector.[10]

Fuch's second detailed discussion concerns productivity in barber and beauty shops. The measurement of output in this service provides a classic example of the direct output method. Current dollar receipts of barber and beauty shops are deflated by a price index developed for these services. The underlying assumption is that the haircut or the permanent wave is a relatively standard activity with little variation in quality. The price index is simply the ratio of the current price to the base period price of that standard service. If the service is not standard in quality, such a price index will not adequately reflect real price changes. It will overestimate the price change and underestimate the real quantity change. Using this procedure, Fuchs finds that productivity in the beauty shop has increased, whereas in the barber shop it has remained relatively constant because technology has improved in the beauty shop but has remained relatively constant in the barber shop. The technological revolution that occurred in barbering, the safety razor, moved the shaving function into the home. Thus, according to this method of measurement, it did not result in increased barber productivity.[11]

Carolyn Shaw Bell has argued that the problem here is with the method; it does not measure the real productivity change that has occurred. When regarded from the viewpoint of results (i.e., clean, well-groomed faces), productivity has increased greatly. Bell believes that the results-oriented or object-function method is the proper way to estimate productivity. She feels that if such a method were used, the estimated productivity of barbers would show large increases. Even in the relatively simple case of barbering, there is no general agreement on the proper method for estimating output.[12]

The third and perhaps most interesting case study presented by Fuchs is medical care. Medical care output is the most difficult of the three services; not only is there disagreement over the proper measurement method, there is also disagreement over what actually is to be measured. The traditional method is to take the total dollar receipts of the medical care industry and deflate by a price index based on the cost of "standard" activities such as the cost of an average hospital day or an average visit to the doctor's office. To the extent that hospital days or visits to the doctor's office are not homogeneous over time in quantity or quality, the price index is biased. But the rapid technological change that has occurred in this industry makes it almost impossible to develop a homogeneous price index. Hence many argue that productivity estimates based on this method are too low and estimates of real price increases are too high.[13]

Both criticisms of the direct output approach to productivity measurement apply to its application in the medical care industry. The direct outputs of the service are not homogeneous, and there is no agreement as to how these outputs relate to the overall objectives of health care. The latter point is to some extent a result of the lack of agreement on the overall objectives of health care. Fuchs suggests at least three separate outputs of health care: (1) actual contribution made to the individual's health; (2) evaluation of the individual's present health situation for insurance purposes, and so forth; and (3) other services such as room and board provided by a hospital during a patient's stay.[14] Each of these is separate and theoretically quantifiable. Each also has an effect on overall health care.

Fuchs has suggested that the output of health care could be estimated by first identifying and then measuring changes in the objectives of health care provision. Since health care has multiple objectives, one must first define some set of quantifiable proxies which will estimate changes in the effects of health services and therefore the overall level of health care. The usual procedure is to develop negative proxies; the level of health is defined in terms of rates of mortality, morbidity, disability, and so forth. According to the proponents of this approach, changes in these proxies, after proper adjustment for changes in quality, may be used as estimates of changes in the output of private health care.[15]

To date, no studies of private sector service productivity have used this method to estimate changes in output. It is very difficult to separate changes in those proxies resulting from changes in the actual quantity of the service provided from changes which result from other environmental factors, i.e., urbanization of lifestyle or level of education, which also impact on health care. A second problem with this approach is that it would require an almost endless list of proxies to accurately reflect all aspects of private health care.[16]

Based on this and other research, Fuchs provides estimates of changes in both employment and productivity for the agricultural, industrial, and service sectors of the economy. Table 3-3 summarizes these estimates. General government is included as a part of the service sector but is separately identified in the summary tables. Employment in services grew at an average annual rate of 2.0 percent for the period 1929-65, as compared to 1.2 percent for industry and −2.3 percent for agriculture. Service employment also showed the fastest rate of growth for each of the separately identified subperiods.

After providing some tentative explanations for this shift in employment toward services, Fuchs concludes that the primary reason is the low rate of productivity increase in this sector. A part of the shift, he explains, may be attributed to differences in expenditure elasticity. He estimates the income elasticity of expenditures for services at 1.12 percent while that for goods at only 0.93 percent.[17] A 1 percent increase in personal income generates a 1.12 percent increase in expenditure on services, and a 0.93 percent increase in expenditure on goods. A second contributing factor is that there has been a greater decline in hours worked in the service sector than in either industry or agriculture. But these differences are not sufficient to explain the relative magnitude of the shifts in employment. Fuchs concludes that the primary explanation for these shifts lies in the fact that productivity has grown less rapidly in services than in either industry or agriculture. In the service sector, the capital/output ratio is lower and has increased at a slower rate than in goods production. The quality of labor as measured by the level of schooling, the age, and the percentage male appears to be lower in the service sector than in goods production, resulting in less "embodiment" of human capital in service production.[18] As a result, productivity in the service area during the postwar period has

public sector.[22] Shoup suggests a deductive estimation of cost functions for public services. His approach explicitly recognizes geographic area served as a cost factor. Although this approach has not been empirically tested, it does offer some interesting possibilities for estimating changes in public sector output. These three studies are examined in greater detail in the latter part of this chapter.

Measuring Outputs by Measuring Inputs

The least sophisticated but most popular method of estimating the quantity of public services is to measure the value of the inputs that go into those services. If the value of the inputs making up a particular service is $100, the estimated value of the output of that service is $100. If the value of these inputs increases by $10, the value of the output of that service automatically increases by $10. The general assumption underlying this method is that no value is added by the public sector. It is analogous to estimating the value of the output of the automobile industry by measuring the factor cost of the labor and capital that went into producing cars, an approach which all would agree is unacceptable. With this method, productivity (by definition) cannot change. Except for statistical discrepancies, the value of public sector output must equal the value of the inputs generating those outputs.

The Determinants Approach

Another popular approach used to analyze the public sector is the determinants approach. This method employs expenditures, either total or per capita, rather than factor costs to estimate output. The basic justification for using expenditures is that they provide an index of the level of service rendered. As Sacks and Ranney have argued in their study of suburban education:

the resources used for public education are taken as an index of the level of service being provided and the effort which this level requires. The measures used reflect two aspects of the nature of suburban education. One is the educational aspect which involves the provision of a certain level or quality of education. In spite of its limitations, the best single measure of the level of education is current educational expenditures per student. While this is not a perfect measure, it does provide a reasonable means of quantifying the level of education being provided.[23]

Multiple regression analysis with expenditures as the dependent variable and any factor which may influence the level of that expenditure—including proxies representing quality changes—as the independent variable, is the technique used to implement this approach. Either time-series or cross-section data may be used. The purpose of this type of analysis is to identify and estimate the importance of those factors that determine the level of expenditure of a particular governmental function. Using determinants analysis, differences in the expenditure levels of different units of government can be explained.

Two methodological problems impede the use of this method as a valid approach for estimating changes in the numerator of a productivity ratio. First, there is the problem of identification. Since the concept of productivity concentrates on the supply and the production process, it depends upon the ability to hypothesize both production and cost functions, and therefore independent supply curves. The independent variables, the so-called determinants, affect both the demand for, and the supply of, public services. For example, income is both a determinant of the demand for a particular public service and a determinant of the tax revenue available to finance that service. The inability to separately identify demand and supply variables makes it impossible to specify either demand or supply equations. Inferences that can be drawn from changes in productivity ratios deal primarily with supply relationships. Independent estimates of supply variables are important. The inability to make these estimates weakens this method's applicability for productivity measurement.

The second problem is the lack of an adequate behavioral theory underlying this type of analysis. For the private sector such a theory exists, based on maximization of profits by the businessman and maximization of utility by the consumer. For the public sector there is no simple behavioral theory. As a result the independent variables included in the model and the parameters that are estimated often lack theoretical justification.

Determinants studies are useful for explaining differences in levels of expenditures either over time or among units of government. But because of the problems outlined above, they do not provide useful estimates of changes in public sector output for productivity analysis.[24]

Measuring Consequences

Measuring the quantity of governmental output by measuring the effects of that output is a method which has gained a good deal of popularity recently. This method begins by asserting that it is the consequences of the service that reflect consumer demand. Each public service has a number of expected consequences or results. The goals of the public service are those expected consequences, usually broadly defined, and are, according to the logic of this method, of primary interest to the citizenry. For example, fire and police services are demanded for protection, trash collection is demanded for cleanliness, and education is demanded for a more literate citizenry.

The first step in this procedure is to designate quantifiable dimensions of these expected results as proxies for public service output. These expected consequences have multiple dimensions, each representing some aspect of the overall goal. Any number of these dimensions may be used as output proxies. Test scores, number of students going to college, the dropout rate, or even changes in the distribution of income resulting from a more open educational system, all represent different results from the educational system and may be used as proxies for educational output. Crime statistics by category may be a proxy for police protection. Death rates, reductions in communicable diseases or infant mortality may be used as proxies for health care. Changes in output are then estimated from changes in these proxies after the proxies have been "appropriately" adjusted for quality changes.[25]

This methodology is useful for certain types of studies, particularly for program evaluation and hence for public expenditure justification. To evaluate public programs and to justify public budgets, it is very important to establish program goals and to develop quantifiable proxies to measure progress toward such goals. The method does not provide a useful framework for measuring the quantity of public sector output in the terms necessary for productivity studies. Products of the production process are confused with the consequences or effects of those products. Even though final or true consumer demand may be for these consequences, it is still analytically quite useful to separate the outputs of the production process from the consequences of the outputs.

Kelvin Lancaster, in what he has termed a new approach to consumer theory, has argued that the demand for privately provided goods and services is in reality a demand not for the goods or services themselves but rather for the characteristics associated with those goods and services.[26] "Goods, as such, are not the immediate objects of preference or utility or welfare, but have associated with them characteristics which are directly relevant to the consumer."[27] He adds that the "consumer's demand for goods arises from the fact that goods are required to obtain characteristics and is a derived demand."[28] In this view, goods are "inputs into a process in which these characteristics are the outputs."[29] Even if this view of demand is accepted, production theory has been able to make numerous advances by separating product from consequences.

Production theory hypothesizes relationships between inputs and products regardless of the use of physical or psychological characteristics generic to those products. If one examines the manufacture of guns, production theory allows one to make hypotheses regarding the relationship between the quantities of labor and capital used in the production process and the quantity of guns of a given quality which come out of that production process. The theory does not question how those guns are used. It does not allow hypotheses to be drawn regarding the number of animals or people that may be killed because of the production of guns. Production theory has increased our understanding of the production process. Productivity measurement and the inferences which can be drawn from it regarding shifts in the production function, economic growth, and changes in price all rest on this approach and its requirements of independent measures of quantities produced.

There is no reliable linkage between inputs and consequences. Without such a linkage, it is very difficult to draw inferences from changes in ratios of consequences to inputs. Is that relationship normally stable? What does it mean to say that consequences, however measured, have grown at a faster rate than inputs? If productivity is defined as the ratio of consequences to inputs, then a change in productivity takes on a new meaning that is difficult to conceptualize. The aggregation of differing consequences for different households and attaching weights thereto is most evidently an elusive matter.

Using measures of consequences as measures of output in an attempt to estimate changes in productivity confuses efficiency with effectiveness. As was discussed in Chapter 2, efficiency measures one aspect of the production process while effectiveness measures another. The results of these two measures are not necessarily the same. The efficiency of providing a service may improve while at the same time that service's effectiveness may fall. Or the effectiveness of the service may improve while efficiency may fall.

Consider education in 1950 and in 1970 as an example. Assume that output is measured in terms of test scores—a consequence. Also assume that inputs in terms of labor and capital remain constant. Child A enters the system in the first grade in 1950 and at the end of twelve years scores the equivalent of twelfth grade on a standard test. Child B enters the system in 1970. Because of changes in environmental factors—for example, his exposure to Sesame Street—this child enters with the equivalent score of a 1950 third grader. At the end of twelve years, he also scores at the twelfth grade level. Finally, child C enters the system in 1970, again with a third grade equivalent score. At the end of twelve years, this child scores the equivalent of the fourteenth grade.

What has happened to our system in terms of efficiency and effectiveness? If output is measured in terms of results for child B, the efficiency of the system has fallen between 1950 and 1970. Using the same quantity of labor and capital, the system was only able to move the child from the third to the twelfth grade, as compared to 1950 when the child moved from the first to the twelfth grade. The effectiveness of the system has not changed in that in both 1950 and 1970 the end result was a twelfth grade test score. Using the same kind of argument, in case C, the efficiency of the system has not improved from 1950 whereas the effectiveness has, in that the child now reaches grade fourteen in his test score. Thus these two measures do not necessarily provide the same results. If proxies for consequences are to be used as estimates of output to measure efficiency, these proxies must be adjusted for any changes in environment which may impact on the consequences, a most difficult task.

There are two other points concerning the use of consequences as estimates of output. First, there are negative as well as positive consequences. If consequences are to be used, proxies for negative as well as positive consequences must be included as a part of the estimates. Second, the desired consequences change over time. Such a change is the equivalent of a new product entering the system. The estimates that are developed must be capable of adjustment for such changes in desired results.

Estimating changes in output from changes in consequences can be used for measuring changes in effectiveness, but this is not a very suitable method for measuring changes in efficiency. Productivity estimates require an intermediate step and that step is the estimate of quantities of direct outputs. As Burkhead and Miner have explained,

the quantity of services performed by governments (streets patrolled, classes conducted) are analogous to the quantities of services performed by private producers (concerts given, hospital days provided). Measures of the effects of the provision of these services are important, and indeed determine their valuation, but are not themselves measures of quantity. . . . Why should the quantity of preventive services provided by governments be conceived of in terms of reduction in incidence of unwanted activities when private services are not marketed in accordance with such measures? Tempting as it is to go from expenditure to consequence, economics has profited greatly from the intermediate step of specification of units of output and their cost.[30]

The PPBS Approach

A method receiving a great deal of recent attention is the planning-programming-budgeting system approach to public sector budgeting, and therefore to public sector output measurement. "PPBS," as it has come to be called, has a long history dating back to the 1912 Taft Commission on Economy and Efficiency.[31] It gained national prominence in 1961 with its adoption by the Department of Defense under Robert McNamara and by all federal agencies in 1965.[32] It is also being tried at present as a budgeting method in many state and local governments.

In general, the goal of PPBS may be described as an "attempt to measure, in systems terms, the relationships between inputs and ouputs."[33] This general goal may be subdivided into three objectives. First, PPBS provides a classification system. Government programs are classified according to their objectives or goals. Second, PPBS evaluates programs by comparing program results with program costs. In the process it provides a mechanism for evaluating alternative methods of achieving the same results. Finally, PPBS aids in long-range program planning.

The concern here is primarily with the second objective of PPBS analysis because, to make the kind of evaluation called for, some definition of program output is called for. PPBS analysis normally employs the consequences method for estimating changes in program output with these consequences or results often very broadly defined. To illustrate, Robert N. Grosse reports on an evaluation of alternative ways of improving child health care. The goal of the program was "to make needed maternal and child health services available and accessible to all, in particular to all expectant mothers and children in depressed areas."[34] Two consequences were agreed upon as proxies for program outputs: mortality prevention and the prevention or correction of physical handicaps. These two proxies were quantified in the following terms:

Maternal deaths prevented
Premature births prevented
Infant deaths prevented
Mental retardation prevented
Handicaps prevented or corrected by age 18:
　　All
　　Amblyopia
Hearing Loss:
　　All
　　Binaural
Other physical handicaps.[35]

In his discussion of the application of benefit-cost analysis to public expenditure and program evaluation analysis, Robert H. Haveman carries the consequences approach to its logical extreme by simply defining all favorable results as program outputs.

The first task in applying benefit-cost analysis to a proposed undertaking is to isolate the full set of impacts, both favorable and unfavorable, which it generates. The favorable effects can be labelled outputs and the unfavorable ones inputs.[36]

He adds that "once these values are placed on inputs and outputs, they become known as costs and benefits."[37]

Although PPBS' use of the consequences method is appropriate for certain types of program evaluation, even when carried to the extreme that Haveman has suggested, it does not provide an estimate of output suitable for productivity ratios. It suffers from the lack of a general theoretical link connecting consequences and direct outputs and inputs, and it confuses efficiency and effectiveness. Program costs and governmental productivity change for a number of reasons. The consequences method as it is employed by PPBS is not capable of discriminating among those reasons.

Measuring Direct Outputs

Direct outputs are the end products of public services production; they are what is actually provided. The educational system, for example, actually provides so many classroom hours of a given subject material, the police service provides so many blocks patrolled or so many policemen directing traffic. This method involves identifying the major activities performed in the provision of each service, quantifying these activities and adjusting them for quality changes, and finally estimating changes in their quantity.

In their study of local government costs, Bradford, Malt, and Oates draw a clear conceptual distinction between direct outputs and consequences.[38] They begin by separating output into what they term "D-output," "the services directly produced" and "C-output," "the thing or things of primary interest to the citizen-consumer,"[39] in other words, the consequences. Although only the C-output of a particular service enters into the utility function of the consumer, it is functionally dependent upon the D-output of that service, upon the D-output of any other public service that may influence it, and upon any environmental factors that may influence it. Their example concerning police explains this distinction.

Let I represent a vector of inputs in the production of a public good. Various types and combinations of labor, capital equipment, etc., as expressed in the vector I, map through a production function into a vector D of "directly produced" goods or services. In the case of police services, for example, the components of I would presumably consist of such inputs as men, cars, and communications systems; the resulting vector D of direct outputs might include as components the number of city blocks provided with a specified degree of surveillance (by patrolmen on foot or automobile patrols), the number of blocks provided with readily available police-officer reserves, the number of intersections provided with traffic control, and so on.

However, the authors point out that when

... the citizen votes on a police budget, however, he is primarily interested, not in the vector D, but rather in such things as the degree of safety from criminal activity and the smoothness and rapidity of the flow of traffic. And these depend only in part on D. ... This vector is, moreover, completely determined by the vector D and by certain environmental variables, such as the "propensity to riot" in the community and the driving habits of local residents. Let C be such a vector.[40]

It is important to maintain this distinction between these two types of output because the costs of D versus the costs of C proceed at different rates and are influenced by different factors. Environmental characteristics of cities may make it now much more costly to provide a specific level of C-output than it was in the past, whereas these same environmental factors may have no influence on the cost of providing D-output. One may meaningfully discuss scalar multiples of D-output in the traditional economic sense. If the quantity of inputs is doubled, and direct output more than doubles, economies of scale exist. The quantity of C, however, is the result of a number of influences, and it is not meaningful to talk in the traditional sense about a scalar multiple of C. On the other hand, as Bradford, Malt, and Oates have argued:

What we can examine, however, is the cost of making C available to an increased number of persons. In this second sense, "economies of scale" are present if C, for instance, can be provided for twice as many consumers without doubling the quantities of inputs.[41]

In examining productivity in the public sector, the output concept closest to that used in the private sector is output directly produced—the D-output in the above terminology. These are the activities actually performed by the public sector; they are the quantities that come out of the production pipeline. Note that even when this distinction is recognized and maintained, all of the problems associated with measuring public sector output are not resolved and Bradford, Malt and Oates have pointed this out.

Even when the distinction between the D- and C- concepts of output is carefully drawn and maintained, a multi-dimensional vector of output remains, with variations over time and space in the relative sizes of components; the perennial problem of quality change.[42]

This is, of course, true. To get comparable units of output over time and space, units must be adjusted for changes in quality. But by differentiating between the D and C concepts and by concentration on D-output, the quality adjustment problem becomes similar to the problem of quality change which must be faced in analyzing the private sector. Some of the same techniques developed to solve this problem in the private sector may possibly be applied to the public sector.

This method requires an assumed relationship between direct outputs and those consequences demanded by the citizen-taxpayer. It has been criticized on the ground that such a direct connection does not exist, that these direct outputs are of little concern to the consumer and are of little consequence. This kind of an argument often proceeds by pointing out that both the actual and demanded consequences of public programs have experienced large changes over time, whereas the direct outputs of the public sector have changed relatively little. For example, it may be argued that what is demanded from a school system has changed drastically since the beginning of the century. The earlier school system was to provide some reading and writing skills and very little else. One's occupation was learned at home. Now citizens demand much more of the modern school system. The school either must provide the student with occupational training or must prepare him to continue within the system to the next level where such training will be provided. Schools must perform a function that was previously performed in the home; yet the direct outputs of the school system have not radically changed.

One logical extension of this kind of argument is that much of the dissatisfaction currently expressed in our urban areas is due to a change in the demand for consequences, accompanied by little or no change in the direct outputs provided by urban governments. City governments may be very good at providing basic service functions. But now citizens are no longer demanding a limited range of local government functions. Their demands are for a reduction in racism, increased employment opportunities, and environmental improvement. The activities of local government, on the other hand, continue to be directed to the provision of basic services. Thus there is a mismatch between direct outputs and those consequences demanded by the citizen-taxpayer. Analyzing direct outputs, it is argued, therefore misses the whole problem and is not really significant.

There are two basic difficulties with such an argument. First, if one returns to Lancaster's approach, one finds that the same assumption of a connection between goods and "sources of utility" must be made as for the private sector. To argue that such a mismatch occurs in the public sector but not in the private sector, one must provide a palatable reason for the difference. One may argue that choices are greater in the private sector, or that choices are made directly in the private sector, whereas in the public sector they are made indirectly through the voting process. Either contention makes a number of implicit assumptions concerning the democratic process, all of which must be justified, and some of which are rather repugnant—for example, that local government is inherently irresponsible and nonresponsive.

The second problem with the above argument is that it confuses efficiency and effectiveness. It is an effectiveness argument being applied to a method of measuring output for estimates of efficiency. Separating effectiveness and efficiency has proved most helpful in private sector analysis; it should be likewise for the public sector.

There are other criticisms of this method that are much more valid even if less devastating. For instance, the method is incomplete in that it cannot take into account a number of functions performed by government such as providing identity to the citizens or enhancing their feelings of community. The method does not solve the problem of quality adjustment. Yet it does provide a unit that can be adjusted, and this is at least a step in the right direction. Direct outputs of the public sector are closest to the type of output unit required by production theory They are the most appropriate unit of measurement for productivity analysis.

The Production Function Approach

The production-function approach is concerned with analyzing the reasons for changes in public sector output. The general procedure is to postulate a production function for a given public service. Any of the three methods previously discussed may be used to generate output proxies for the postulated function. Using multiple regression analysis, the coefficients of the production function are then estimated and analyzed. Theoretically, using such a procedure, productivity estimates may be generated, and economies of scale for public functions and cost and supply curves may be estimated.

Werner Hirsch hypothesizes such a general production function as follows: $0 = f(I,S,T)$ where $0 = AQ$.[43] In this sense, I equals the input factors, land, labor, and capital. S equals service conditions affecting input requirements. These may include items such as legal, political, or environmental factors affecting the quantity of services provided, such as the placing of fire hydrants, the structural material used in building in the area, or the number of buildings with their own individual sprinkler systems. For education, Hirsch would also like to include the native ability of the children in the system as a part of the service requirement. "In relation to education, a child's native ability as well as his motivation and desire to learn can be looked upon as conditions affecting the ease or difficulty with which a given achievement can be accomplished."[44] The inclusion of factors such as this may or may not be appropriate for a production function. First, many of these factors are extremely difficult to quantify. Second, to be included, each factor needs theoretical justification. Finally, determining which of these service conditions should be included as a functional variable depends upon what is being measured. If one's goal is to measure direct outputs, then the inclusion of a child's native ability has no place unless such ability can be related to the activity being measured.

T is the state of technology—again a difficult variable to quantify and include in the function. Hirsch feels that this variable has been relatively stable over time.

In this function, A is the quantity of output and Q is the quality of output. Although Hirsch recognizes the difficulties involved in estimating the quantity of output, he feels that these difficulties are not unique to the public sector. As far as he is concerned, A may be estimated from proxies of either changes in direct outputs or consequences. He does not differentiate between these different types of output, nor does he seem to think that such a differentiation is necessary.

Since price is not available for public sector services, the implication here is that quality proxies should be developed which can be multiplied by A to yield an estimate of total output. Later in the same discussion, Hirsch suggests that this function may be rewritten as follows: $A = f(Q, I, S, T)$.[45] In this case, the quality proxy or proxies are a part of the independent variables and the effects of variations in quality on the quantity of output may be estimated.

Based on this formulation, Hirsch estimates the output of residential refuse collection for twenty-four St. Louis city-county municipalities in 1960.[46] His basic estimating equation is

$$0 = \sum_{i=1}^{n} A_i Q_i$$

where A_i is the number of full refuse containers collected per year; Q_i is the "dollar value of the ith quality per basic service unit, e.g., in terms of dollar costs"[47]—which must be estimated from another regression equation; and 0 is output in terms of dollar costs. As he admits, his example is for "a relatively simple urban public service."[48]

Hirsch's method is most useful in the area of services where there is an easily definable unit of output—for example, in his own study of trash collection. This method does not solve the problem of quantifying output for the more difficult and, in general, the more important services provided by government—for example, education.

Estimating production functions for those public services where quantities of output are difficult to measure—in other words, most public services—has proved to be a formidable task. An ambitious attempt in this direction was undertaken by Burkhead, Fox, and Holland in their study of education in Chicago and Atlanta,[49] and similar approaches have been used by others. Their study used a production function to estimate the effects of specific inputs on the outputs of the educational system. Educational output was defined in terms of goals, generally stated as a "desired behavioral capability."[50] This general goal is divided into two subcategories: increases in skills and learning ability, and socialization. IQ, reading and writing test scores, post-high school education, and dropout rates were all used as proxies for these two outputs in Chicago. For Atlanta, IQ, verbal and quantitative test scores, dropout rates, post high school education, and post-high school employment were used as output proxies.

Inputs were divided into three categories: status variables which were primarily socioeconomic in character, basic input variables which included average daily membership and age of school building, and process variables which indicated factor combinations that might affect educational output. These process variables are policy parameters; they estimate the effects on output of combining input factors in different ways—for example, varying the class size. Their production function takes the general form of $0 = f(S, I, P)$.[51] The estimating procedure used was step-order multiple regression. Generally the authors found that for both cities factors external to the school system, mainly socioeconomic factors, were the major determinants of school performance.

It will be recalled that productivity measurement relates the value added by the production process to the quantity of inputs used in that process. In the second half of their study, Burkhead, Fox, and Holland used their production function to estimate the value added by the school system. Here they attempted "to explain what the input and process variables contribute to learning beyond that expected as a consequence of the status variables."[52] To estimate value added, ninth grade IQ scores were used to predict eleventh grade test scores for Chicago, and the residuals, the value added, were then analyzed. For Atlanta, eighth grade IQ scores were used to predict tenth grade verbal test scores and again the residuals were analyzed.

In Chicago, two variants of the original regression model were used to analyze eleventh grade reading score residuals. In variant I of the model, income is entered as the first independent variable whereas in variant II income is not entered until later in the step order regression. The purpose of variant II is to de-emphasize the importance of income. Teacher experience proved to be the single most important explanatory variable, and it was positive. In other words, teacher experience was most important in explaining the difference between the actual eleventh grade reading score and the score predicted by ninth grade IQ. In Atlanta only variant I of the model was tried. Here, the teacher turnover rate proved to be the only significant variable in determining the value added and its influence was negative. A high turnover rate meant lower value added on verbal test scores.

The production function approach to analyzing the public sector has proved to be most useful when applied to the "hard" services where a unit of output is directly available. In these services, output can be measured in terms of units that are directly produced, i.e., number of tons of trash collected per day. For these services, the major problem is one of making the appropriate quality adjustments.

When this approach is applied to the area of social services, proxies for consequences have been used to estimate changes in output. These proxies estimate changes in the C-vector rather than the D-vector. The primary problem in this case is the lack of a theory which relates inputs to consequences. As Burkhead, Fox, and Holland frankly point out, the missing link in their study is an adequate learning theory which would relate educational consequences and the inputs into the educational system. Without this theoretical link, instead of having a functional relationship from which inferences can be drawn and parameters estimated, one has only an input-output equation about which all that can be said is that certain input factors influence consequences. One is prevented from hypothesizing as to how or why.

Shoup's Approach

Carl Shoup has suggested a deductive approach to the estimation of cost functions for public services.[53] Concentrating on three variables, number of persons served, geographic area served, and number of service units provided, Shoup hypothesizes marginal, average, and total cost curves for both group consumer goods, which are collectively consumed (one person's consumption does not reduce the quantity available to another person), and group consumer goods, which are noncollectively consumed (one person's consumption does reduce the quantity available for another person). His procedure is first to hold area served constant and examine the variations in cost when number of persons served and number of units supplied are allowed to vary. He then holds number of persons supplied constant and allows area served and number of units supplied to vary. Applying this methodology to certain individual functions, Shoup concludes that the effects on cost of the traditionally used independent factors vary, depending upon the specific function under study and the technology used to provide that function.

Although Shoup's method has not as yet been empirically tested, it may prove to be quite helpful in the estimation of cost functions and therefore in improving productivity. It does explicitly introduce area served as an important variable affecting cost. The problem with this approach is that it requires an independent estimate of output quantities, and Shoup sheds little light on how that estimate is to be derived.

Summary

The major impediment to public-sector productivity analysis is the lack of independent estimates of the quantity and quality of governmental output. This section has been devoted to an examination of the general methods that have been suggested as possible ways of overcoming this impediment. Three methods for measuring public sector output have been discussed: estimating output quantity and quality from estimates of inputs, consequences, and direct outputs. Each of these methods has its own particular drawbacks. The method closest to providing estimates analogous to measures for the private sector is the direct output approach. But even this method does not solve the problem of changes in quality, and using this method to measure local government productivity confronts a second, more practical obstacle. Most local governments do not regularly collect data on direct outputs. Thus at the local level, information on changes in direct outputs over time is simply not available.

Even with these problems, there have been some studies aimed at measuring public sector productivity, in particular federal government productivity. The next chapter examines these studies to see how successful they have been.

4 Empirical Studies

The absence of reliable quantitative and conceptual estimates of public sector output has greatly limited the volume of empirical studies of public sector productivity. Yet, as is often the case, the lack of empirical work in this area has not hindered intuitive speculation regarding changes in public sector productivity by either the professional economist or the layman. The layman's intuitive impression is normally rather straightforward. In his view, government is simply inefficient. Translated into technical terms, he is suggesting that productivity in the public sector has at best not kept pace with private sector productivity gains. At worst, it has actually fallen. The professional economist has not been able to provide the empirical analysis necessary to either support or counter this popular view of changes in government productivity.

The impressionistic pronouncements of the professional economist regarding changes in government productivity vary between those who feel that productivity at all levels of government has increased, to those who believe that there has been very little if any increase. For example, in his study of trends in government activity, Solomon Fabricant suggests that since the beginning of the century productivity at all levels of government has increased.[1] He believes that this increase has been the result of improvements in both technology and in public administration practices. The technological improvements have come primarily in the form of improvements in capital equipment; for example, new machines for cancelling and postmarking letters, the replacement of horse-drawn with motorized vehicles in city police departments, and so forth. A number of improvements have also occurred in public administration practices. Fabricant points to three as of primary importance in increasing productivity: the introduction of the merit system, the increased use of centralized purchasing, and the consolidation of some units of government resulting in economies of scale.

Although Fabricant feels that government productivity has increased, he refuses to speculate as to whether or not that growth has been more or less rapid than private sector productivity improvement.

Whether government productivity rose more or less rapidly than productivity in private enterprise is another matter, and one on which lack of information makes it idle to speculate. . . . To hold that government productivity probably has advanced does not imply an opinion about its absolute level or the relation of that level to the level in private business. Whether government is more or less efficient than nongovernment enterprise is another important question, but one not immediately relevant to the matter under discussion, and in any case not answerable with the data we have considered.[2]

59

Baumol, on the other hand, speculates on just that point.[3] His model is that service sector productivity has increased, if at all, at a much slower pace than goods sector productivity. If this assumption is combined with the assumption that wage rates are set in the goods sector, the result is both a continued shift in employment from the goods to the services area and a continued increase in the relative cost of services. The Baumol prediction, that of ever-increasing relative costs, spells dangerous consequences for local governments. Although some empirical studies of changes in government productivity have been done, Baumol does not appeal to them for justification of his view, and Fabricant uses them only for purposes of drawing examples of technological changes.

The purpose of this chapter is to review and evaluate the empirical studies of public sector productivity that have been done. Studies of federal government productivity are examined first. The second part of this chapter examines studies of changes in state and local government productivity.

Methodology

The basic methodology used in empirical studies of federal government productivity has remained remarkably constant. The first step is to identify those organizations within the federal government to be studied. The choice depends upon the availability of reliable output measures for the organization. Since for many agencies output measures are not available, none of the studies have included the entire federal bureaucracy. The most ambitious covers less than 60 percent of federal civilian employees and none have attempted to include military operations.

As a part of this procedure, organizational outputs must be identified and quantified. In general, to qualify for selection, the output must meet most or all of the following criteria. First, to avoid double counting, the outputs selected must be easily counted and consistent for the period chosen for study. In other words, data on the outputs must be readily available, quantitatively definable, and uniform over time. Third, the outputs must be mission-oriented in that they directly relate to the purposes of the agency or are a part of the organizational elements of the agency. Finally, the outputs must be final or at least "an intermediate product contributing to the final product."[4] *Final* in this sense may be interpreted in a variety of ways. It may be defined in terms of who receives the product or in terms of whether or not the product is mission-oriented. If either the public or another organization receives the product, it may be considered final. If the product is directly associated with the organization's mission or is directly public-benefit oriented, it also may be considered final.[5]

The second step in this method is to estimate the quantity of inputs associated with each output. Because of the difficulties associated with measuring capital in the federal government, inputs are usually measured in terms of either man-hours or constant-dollar labor costs.

The third step in the process is to weight each output by the percentage of the total inputs used in the production of that output in the base year. Federal government outputs come in a number of forms ranging all the way from watts of electricity generated to number of outpatients served by a hospital clinic. To gauge their relative importance and to make them additive, they must be expressed in terms of a common unit. Weighting outputs by man-hours is one method of determining relative importance. Outputs requiring more man-hours are more important in terms of man-hour resources used and are given greater weights. The weighting process also provides a common unit of measure such that these diverse outputs can be added.

For example, in the 1964 study of government productivity, the Division of Disbursements, Department of the Treasury, identified two outputs—checks processed and bonds processed.[6] In 1962, the base year, 317,662 checks were processed while 3,999 bonds were processed; 1,644 man-years of labor were paid for processing these checks and bonds. Of these, 1,579 were involved in the processing of bonds. The calculated weight for checks was 0.005 (1,579 divided by 317,662) while that for bonds was 0.016 (65 divided by 3,999). The units of outputs, the checks and bonds, were multiplied by their base-year weight. Both checks and bonds are now in terms of man-years paid and may be added.[7]

The final step in this process is to express both output and input as indexes. Dividing the output index by the input index yields an index of productivity.

This general methodology has been employed in all studies of federal government productivity. The major difficulty is the lack of attention to changes in the quality of output. All of the studies recognize the need for making quality adjustments, yet none do. Although this situation is a result of inadequate estimates of federal government output rather than of the method itself, it does mean that to the extent quality has changed, the method yields rather unreliable results.

Federal Government Studies

The U.S. Postal Service

The first empirical study of productivity in the federal government was done by Witt Bowden in 1932.[8] He examined the United States Postal Service for the years 1908-1931, omitting 1909, 1911, and 1913-25. Bowden identified thirteen separate Postal Service outputs: seven different classes of mail and six types of special-service transactions. To add these seven different classes of mail, he attempted to weight each class by the relative average labor time required to handle units of that class as compared to the average labor time required to handle a first-class letter. The labor time required to handle a first-class letter was set equal to one. If it took three times as much labor time to handle a fourth-class newspaper, each unit of fourth-class mail was weighted by three.

Because of limited data, Bowden was able to estimate separate weights only for fourth-class mail. All other classes were given a weight of one. Based on extensive tests done by the Post Office Department, fourth-class mail was given a weight of three for the years 1908, 1910, and 1912. The Parcel Post System was introduced in 1913 and the size and weight of parcels were greatly increased. For the period 1926-31 Bowden used a weighting factor of 8.2 for this class of mail.[9]

Changing his labor-weighting factor in the middle of the study distorts Bowden's estimates of output, probably resulting in an overestimation of output and hence an overestimation of productivity increase. If fourth-class mail is basically the same during the two periods, a weight of three should have been used throughout the study. The increase in labor time required to handle this class of mail during the latter part of the study would then have appeared as a decline in productivity rather than as an increase in output. If fourth-class mail was significantly different, in other words, if it was really a new product after 1913, then to combine the two different products Bowden should have used some type of linking adjustment so as not to distort the estimates.[10]

Six classes of special-service transactions were also identified as outputs. Finding it impossible to estimate labor time per transaction, Bowden used the average cost per transaction relative to the average cost of a unit of first-class mail as his output weights. Each of the six special-service transaction classes received a weight. These weights ranged from 5.2 for insurance transactions to 156.0 for postal-savings accounts. Since labor cost is the predominant cost element in both first-class mail handling and in the special-service transactions, Bowden argued that this method is equivalent to weighting by labor time and therefore these two types of output are additive.

Estimates of output were not available for all of the years covered by the study for three types of special-service transactions. The number of COD transactions and insurance transactions were not available until 1926, while the number of depositors with postal-savings accounts was not available until 1912. Bowden handled this problem by simply adding in the new output estimates as they became available. As a result, his index of special-service transactions jumped from 121.1 in 1912 to 385.7 in 1926. Including new products in this way overestimates output increases.[11]

Bowden used equivalent full-time postal employees as his estimate of inputs. Based on the number of hours actually paid, he corrected part-time employees to full-time equivalents, but he did not correct for changes in hours worked. During the period 1908-12, many employees were required to work both overtime and Sundays without extra pay. These hours were not included as a part of the estimate of labor input. During the latter period of the study, much of this overtime was worked by part-time employees, paid for, and thus included as a part of labor input. Not correcting for this change overstates the increase in labor input and therefore results in an underestimate of productivity increase.

Bowden also left out certain types of labor. The primary types of labor not included were contract workers and clerks in contract stations. The number of contract workers declined over the period studied, and their work was taken over by full-time employees. By leaving out the contract workers, labor input is underestimated in the base year and the increase in labor is overestimated. Again the result is to bias productivity estimates downward.[12]

Bowden concluded that over the period 1908-31 labor productivity in the United States Postal Department increased by 63.4 percent—an annual increase of 2.15 percent. This was a reasonably impressive improvement.[13]

Although by present standards Bowden's research is not very sophisticated, his basic methodology has been used in all of the studies of federal government productivity since that time. The coverage in the more recent studies has increased, but there have been surprisingly few improvements in the basic methodology. On the whole it is impossible to determine whether Bowden underestimates or overestimates the actual productivity change. His estimates of output lead to an overestimation of productivity, whereas his neglect of some types of labor and the lack of any adjustment for quality improvements leads to an underestimation of productivity change. What Bowden's work does show is that it is possible to estimate public sector productivity. It also lends historical perspective to the more recent studies that are examined.

The Bureau of Land Management

There was little interest in measuring federal government productivity during the depression and the World War II years; the next major study was not published until 1958, when William A. Vogely examined the Bureau of Land Management of the Department of the Interior.[14]

Vogely's primary effort was to devise output measures for the Bureau rather than to measure productivity directly. He divided the Bureau into its major programs—minerals, lands, grazing, and forestry—and identified several output measures for each program. In the process he estimated unit cost measures for minerals, lands, and forestry programs. From these he suggested the direction of productivity changes in each. For the period 1949-54, Vogely found that for minerals and lands programs both man-years per case closed and dollars obligated per case closed fell, indicating increased productivity. For the forestry programs between 1950 and 1954, both man-years and dollars obligated per thousand board feet rose, indicating a decline in productivity. Vogely strongly cautioned against taking these estimates too seriously, suggesting that they might simply be the result of inadequate output estimates. His main conclusion is that "by and large, the outlook for such measurements [output and productivity] is encouraging."[15]

Lytton's Study

In 1959 Henry D. Lytton published his estimates of productivity in the federal government.[16] For the period 1947-58, Lytton estimated productivity indexes for five separate agencies and departments including the Commodity Stabilization Service of the Department of Agriculture, the Social Security Administration of the Department of Health, Education, and Welfare, the Post Office Department, the Veteran's Administration, and the Internal Revenue Service of the Treasury Department. These estimates covered about 56 percent of total federal government non-defense-agency employment located in the United States and included 139 indicators of the work of the federal government. From these he estimated a "tentative" governmentwide productivity index. This index increased by 17.04 percent over the period studied. Put another way, it increased at an average annual compound rate of 1.45 percent. By dropping the estimates for 1958 and not including the medical component of the Veterans' Administration, on the ground that it was not homogeneous with the rest of the services covered, the average annual rate of increase rises to about 2.2 percent, which is not far from the 3.1 percent rate of increase estimated for the private sector for the same period.[17]

It is difficult to evaluate Lytton's study because of the lack of detail describing his index construction. He does not provide the reader with detailed information on the construction of either the output or input indexes. He states that

the usual techniques of weighting and of index-number construction permitted the derivation of the necessary series of indexes to represent the weighted average outputs and the corresponding weighted average productivities of the foregoing seven different cases.[18]

But the "usual" techniques are not described.

Lytton does provide some information on his output indicators. He says that for both the Commodity Stabilization Service and the Social Security Administration he used work measures developed by the agencies themselves. This fact, coupled with a listing of some of the output indicators used, leads one to suspect that some of the outputs may not be final in any sense and that in some cases double-counting may be involved. For example, mail received, personnel, supply, and finance are all listed as outputs of the Department of Veterans Benefits. According to the footnote, all except the mail received are defined as "equivalent veterans-benefits employees (ex-common-service) services."[19] In the case of Veterans Hospitals, the output measure used is the average inpatient load per employee, a measure of questionable value for estimating the output of hospitals in the absence of a quality adjustment. The productivity index developed for Veterans Hospitals declined at an average annual rate of about 1 percent over the period covered.

Lytton also neglected to provide detailed information on the way he weighted the separate outputs so that they could be added. Statements such as "weighted output was estimated by arranging all returns in seven classes, applying fixed weights in most cases and increasing weights in two cases" are not adequately descriptive.[20] Lytton's explanation of the weighting system he used for the outputs of the Internal Revenue Service is not helpful in evaluating his technique.

For the Post Office Department, Lytton basically updated Bowden's original study. During the period 1947-58, productivity in this Department increased by about 13 percent, or at an average annual compound rate of 1.25 percent, as compared to Bowden's finding that from 1908 to 1931 Post Office Department productivity increased by 63.4 percent or 2.15 percent compounded.

Finally, Lytton combined these five indexes into one governmentwide productivity index. Again he neglects to provide any details on exactly how these indexes were combined. For the Commodity Stabilization Service he does not have information prior to 1951. For the Social Security Administration his data begins in 1950, whereas for the other three agencies, his estimates begin with 1947. As discussed earlier, to combine these separate indexes, he should have used some type of linking system.

The fundamental problem with Lytton's estimates of federal government productivity is that he does not provide enough methodological information for an evaluation of his results. How valid or useful his estimates are depends upon the method that he used.

Bureau of the Budget Study

The first major effort at measuring federal government productivity for more than one federal agency began in 1962 under the auspices of the Bureau of the Budget. Interest in such a study began in early 1962 with a five-day conference for senior management analysts on methods of measuring work and productivity.[21] Then, in response to a presidential memorandum issued in late 1962 calling for improved man-power utilization, the Bureau of the Budget asked five agencies—the Treasury Department's Division of Disbursements, the Veterans Administration's Department of Insurance, the Post Office Department, the Systems Maintenance Service of the Federal Aviation Agency, and the Bureau of Land Management of the Department of the Interior, to participate in a study of productivity. This study had three basic goals: to determine (1) which organizations were susceptible to productivity measurement, (2) how it could be measured, and (3) how that measurement could be meaningfully used. The results were published in 1964.[22]

The study covered 24 percent of the total civilian federal employees in the fiscal year 1962. The time period covered varied depending on the particular agency involved. The Division of Disbursement of the Department of the Treasury had the longest coverage—1949-67—while the shortest period covered was from 1958-62 for the Systems Maintenance Service of the Federal Aviation Agency. Because of these differences in time periods covered, no aggregate index was attempted.

Two basic criteria were used for the selection of outputs. First, the output should relate to the mission of the organization as prescribed by either law or established policy. Second, outputs were required to be final. *Final* in this study was defined in terms of who received the service. If the service was received by some person or unit other than the agency providing the service, it was considered final. As a result of these criteria, the outputs identified by each organization varied in number from two for the Division of Disbursement to 318 for the Systems Maintenance Service. The Bureau of Land Management divided its outputs into current outputs, services directly provided to the public, and investment outputs (land and land resource improvements). The Bureau encountered the greatest difficulties in operationally defining their outputs. As a result of these difficulties, the Bureau was able to provide only an interim report at the end of this study and that interim report contained no productivity estimates.[23]

Outputs were adjusted for changes in organizational responsibilities over time, but they were not adjusted for quality changes. Each of the participating agencies was asked to submit a list of quality improvements. For example, the Division of Disbursement pointed to the reduction in check-writing errors as a significant improvement in the quality of the service and the Department of Insurance emphasized the computerization of their system as a major quality improvement in that it provided policyholders with faster, more accurate service. However, none of these quality improvements were incorporated into the empirical estimates of output.[24]

Three separate productivity indexes, output per man-hour, output per constant dollar of payroll cost, and output per constant dollar of total cost, were developed for each of the participating agencies. Three separate weighting systems were developed for each agency. In each case, the weight was the ratio of the number of inputs devoted to a particular output in relation to the total quantity of that output. In only one case, in the Department of Insurance, was it necessary to impute weights.[25] After weighting, the separate outputs for each agency were added and indexed using 1962 as the base year for the index.

Three separate input indexes were developed for each agency. The first was an index of unweighted man-hours. Estimates of actual man-hours worked served as the basis of this index for the Department of Insurance, the Post Office Department, and the Systems Maintenance Service. Full-time equivalent man-years were used by the Division of Disbursement. Dollar payroll cost constituted the second type of input index. This index was calculated by multiplying the number of full-time equivalent man-years worked in each grade for each year by the average fiscal year 1962 personal service cost for that particular grade. The results for all grades were then summed. This procedure was followed by the Division of Disbursement, the Department of Insurance, and the Post Office Department. A simpler method was used in the Systems Maintenance Service. There, increases in pay and fringe benefits were used to adjust personal service costs. This index is equivalent to an index of weighted manpower where the weight is the average 1962 personal service cost for each grade, on the assumption that an upgrading of the work force reflects an increase in the quality of labor.

The third input index calculated for this study was an index of real total budget cost. Although called total budget cost, this index does not truly include all agency costs. For example, all services provided without charge by the General Services Administration were not included. Neither were the overhead charges of the parent agencies (in cases where such costs were applicable), nor were interest charges on capital financing. Each agency developed its own price index to deflate current budget cost. These price indexes were based on parts of the Consumer Price Index, the Wholesale Price Index, and, for certain items, independent calculations.

The results of this study are shown in Table 4-1. The low and high figures are simply the smallest percentage one-year change and the largest percentage one-year change respectively. The average is the annual rate of change. When examining this table, three points should be kept in mind. First, as would be expected from the way the indexes were constructed, productivity as measured by output per man-hour showed the greatest rates of change. Second, because of the different periods covered, it is quite difficult to make meaningful comparisons among the different agencies. The agency with the shortest coverage, the Systems Maintenance Service, also had the only negative average annual rate of increase in output per man-hour. This difference in time periods covered may also help to explain the statement that "productivity change was not correlated with the rate of growth of output."[26] Such a finding is not consistent with what has been found in long-term studies of the private sector. Finally, although the average annual rate of increase of output per man-hour for the Department of Insurance and the Division of Disbursement cannot be rejected solely on the ground that they are too high, they are high enough to be suspect and to require some justification.[27]

It is also interesting to note the average annual rate of change of output per man-hour for the Post Office. For the period 1953-62, the average annual rate of change was only 0.3 percent. This is a much lower rate than the 1.25 percent found in Lytton's study.

Probably the most important finding of this study was that productivity could be estimated and that the estimates could be used. It was possible to make reasonable estimates of government productivity in at least four agencies. In the words of the authors:

Table 4-1
Annual Gains in Productivity of Four Federal Government Organizations: Averages and Dispersion (Percentage per Year)

Organization and Period	Output per Man-Hour			Output per Constant Dollar of Payroll Cost			Output per Constant Dollar of Total Cost		
	Low	Average[a]	High	Low	Average[a]	High	Low	Average[a]	High
Department of Insurance, Veterans Administration, 1955-62	1.1	9.8	23.3	1.0	8.3	25.1	-2.4[b]	6.9[b]	22.4[b]
Division of Disbursement, Department of the Treasury, 1949-62	3.0[c]	9.4[c]	18.4[c]	1.4	8.6	17.5	-1.1[d]	6.1[d]	15.2[d]
Post Office Department, 1953-62	-2.2	0.3	2.5	-2.4	0.2	2.4	-2.5[e]	0.4[e]	3.1[e]
Systems Maintenance Service, Federal Aviation Agency, 1958-62	-11.5	-4.0	2.2	-2.6	.1	3.1	n.a.[f]	n.a.	n.a.

[a]Period averages were calculated by the compound interest formula (annually compounded) applied to the values of the productivity index in the first and last year of the period.

[b]Total budget cost.

[c]Output per man-year.

[d]Excludes postage.

[e]Includes personal services, transportation, and space occupancy costs.

[f]n.a. = not available.

Source: Executive Office of the President, Bureau of the Budget, *Measuring Productivity of Federal Government Organizations* (Washington, D.C.: U.S. Government Printing Office, 1964), p. 14.

As a result of the study, it is believed that development of valid productivity measures is feasible for a considerable proportion of Federal Government activities. The principal obstacle in Government is the requirement that products or services be measurable over a period of time on a consistent basis. Where that is the case productivity measures are not expensive to develop or maintain. This is particularly true if some form of cost accounting or work measurement system is in effect. Finally, it is evident that productivity measurement can be a very useful tool in the management of Government activity in a wide variety of applications, including applications in the budget process.[28]

Although federal government interest in measuring its own productivity lapsed during the mid-1960s, Nestor E. Terleckyj did complete one study during that period.[29] Terleckyj's primary concern was with the types of output and input data available within the federal government, the coverage of that data, and its general quality. As a part of his examination, he updated to 1964 parts of the Bureau of the Budget's study. Table 4-2 shows the results of his update.

In all four cases Terleckyj found much higher average annual rates of productivity change for the period 1961-64 than the BOB had found in their original study. As a result of these higher rates, the average rates for the entire period were increased. Terleckyj was not able to tell whether or not these higher rates indicated a trend in the rate of output per unit of input. He did, however, point out that the two agencies with the fastest average annual rates of productivity increase, the Division of Disbursement and the Insurance Department, were both characterized by radical changes in their production technol-

Table 4-2
Average Annual Rates of Change in Output per Man-Hour

Organization and Period Covered	1961-64 (%)	Period Average (%)
Treasury Department, Division of Disbursement 1949-64	18.4	10.6
Veterans Administration, Insurance Department 1955-64	17.5	11.9
Post Office Department 1953-64	1.1	0.4
Federal Aviation Agency, Systems Maintenance Service 1958-64	4.6	−1.0

Source: Nestor E. Terleckyj, "Recent Trends in Output and Input of the Federal Government," *American Statistical Association, 1964 Proceedings of the Business and Economic Statistics Section* (*General Accounting Office Study*, December 1964), p. 88.

ogy, standardized output, and only a few production locations, whereas the other two agencies have large numbers of locations, diversified output, and little technological change.[30]

Federal government interest in measuring its own productivity was rekindled in September 1970 by a letter from Senator William Proxmire to Elmer Staats, comptroller general of the United States, asking for an "evaluation of the possibilities for measuring productivity in the Federal sector of the economy."[31] the GAO in turn invited the Office of Management and Budget and the Civil Service Commission to join in the project, thus beginning the biggest effort to date toward measuring productivity in the federal government. Seventeen agencies were invited to participate, covering 114 organizational elements and about 56 percent of the civilian employees of these seventeen agencies.

The study was divided into three phases. Phase I consisted of inventorying the current use of quantitative measures within these agencies and determining the percentage of civilian employees covered by the measures. Four types of measures were identified: manpower planning measures, work measures, unit cost measures, and overall productivity measures. Phase I found that 50 percent of the personnel studied were covered by manpower planning measures, 44 percent by work measures, 39 percent by unit cost measures, and only 20 percent by overall productivity measures.[32] Based on these findings, it was decided to continue with phase II.

Phase II had three major objectives. The first objective, coordinated by a team of GAO and BLS specialists, was to develop an overall productivity index based on information compiled from the seventeen agencies. The second objective was to conduct a series of studies and workshops to demonstrate ways in which the use of present measures could be enhanced. This part of the study was coordinated by the Civil Service Commission. The third objective was divided into two parts. The first part, conducted by the GAO, was concerned with special studies aimed at improving capital project planning and unit cost measures. The second part consisted of special studies aimed at improving effectiveness measurement techniques. This part was coordinated by OMB.

Input Measures. In addition to the output information, each agency was asked to submit input data on direct man-years and wage and fringe benefit compensation associated with each output, as well as man-years and compensation associated with nonmeasured outputs.[33] Capital expenditures, other costs, and total expenditures associated with nonmeasured outputs were also requested. The original request was for both input and output data for fiscal years 1958-71. A review of the information submitted indicated that much of it was not available for the earlier years. Thus the actual study was limited to fiscal years 1967-71, using 1967 as the base year.

Data Verification and Adjustment. Although the project team did not actually verify the data submitted by the various agencies, it did ask for support material which would be helpful in both interpreting the indexes and in evaluating the reasonableness of the information. As well as the actual quantity of information, the team requested output definitions, answers to various questions concerning such things as changes in product and quality, and after the index was completed, explanations of any single-year change in productivity of greater than plus or minus 5 percent. Based on this information, twenty-seven submissions covering 38,000 fiscal 1971 man-years were rejected.[34]

Many of the output units used were aggregates of similar but not necessarily identical products. For example "requisitions processed" was used as an output item. Even within the same agency, different types of requisitions are heterogeneous in terms of their man-hours requirements. Changes over time in the mix of products making up any one output item will appear as a change in productivity. If, for example, production shifts from those requisitions requiring a great deal of man-hour effort to those requiring little effort, such a shift will show up as an increase in productivity when in reality only the product mix has changed.

There are two ways to correct for this. One is to further disaggregate the output measure. The second is to check for changes in the mix itself. The project team chose the latter. They requested a typical high and low time for one unit of output. A narrow range indicates a relatively constant product mix, whereas a wide range may indicate that the mix has changed. Some output data was not used because of the wide ranges in production time.

The cycle time required to produce one unit of output was also requested. If that time exceeded one year, the output measure had to be adjusted to reflect what was actually produced that year. The team asked for information on changes in the quality of the output. Few were reported and no adjustments were made to correct for these changes.

Information was also requested on capital expenditure, data sources, and contractor-supported outputs. The capital expenditure information was used to evaluate the impact of investment on productivity. After a short time lag, investment was found to have a favorable impact. The data sources were usually from information already collected by the agencies. Only two contract-produced outputs were included in the measures, and only the government employee time to administer those contracts was included as inputs associated with those outputs.

Finally, information on nonmeasurable activities was requested. The most frequently identified were research and management. In most instances the man-years associated with these nonmeasurable activities were included in the input indexes. These years amounted to about 8 percent of the total man-years.[35]

To further evaluate the output measures, they were divided into four categories: (1) direct outputs, those directly measuring work done; (2) partial outputs, those measuring parts of work done (e.g., hospital patient days); (3) proxy indicators of work done (e.g., patients admitted); and (4) population

result of an increase in output accompanied by a sharp decline in man-years. Such a situation was possible because the number of wage board employees can be adjusted to changes in workload more rapidly than general schedule employees, and because much of the work done by wage board employees was industrial in nature and therefore amenable to the use of labor-saving equipment.[40]

The study does point out that this method is probably not as accurate as the other indexes developed, because some agencies did not precisely differentiate between wage board and general schedule employees.

Finally, productivity indexes were developed by functional classification. There were three functional classifications: (1) *public services*, defined as "process-oriented activities directly benefiting the public"; (2) *internal support services*, defined as "activities performed internally by Government that are necessary for the overall accomplishment of agency missions"; and (3) *industrial activities*, defined as "activities producing or modifying a physical product having some uniqueness of function or design either for internal use by Government or for public use."[41] Each of these functions was then divided into subfunctions with a total of seven subfunctions in all. Organizations were classified into functions and subfunctions according to the activity associated with the largest number of man-years within that organization. Organizations themselves were not divided to fit into the function classed. Table 4-4 shows the distribution of organizational elements, outputs, and man-years covered by function and subfunction. The largest majority of total man-years covered were classified as public service. A majority of these man-years were from the Postal Service. Industrial activities constituted the smallest functional category including only 7.8 percent of the total man-years covered in the sample.

Table 4-5 shows the changes in output per man-year by function and by sub-function and the average annual rate of change for each. The public services category had the smallest productivity gains of the three major functions. Between 1967 and 71, it increased by only 5.1 percent for an average annual rate of change of only 1.3 percent. The authors of the study attribute this slow rate of growth to the fact that outputs within this category are less tangible than in the other categories. Thus there is more chance of an understatement of quality improvements. The authors also point to the fact that there is less opportunity for the use of labor-saving devices within this category.[42] One has difficulty with this explanation because this category is dominated by the Postal Service which has a tangible output. As a matter of fact, Postal Service employees accounted for about 62 percent of the total man-years covered in this category.

Within the public service function, the operating facilities subfunction had the smallest increase in productivity of all the subfunctions studied. Output per unit of input increased by only 3.4 percent over the period studied for an average annual rate of change of only 0.8 percent. Again the Postal Service was

Table 4-4

Distribution of Organizations, Output Measures, and Man-Years by Functional and Subfunctional Classifications, Fiscal Year 1971

Classification	Organizational Elements		Output Measures		Man-Years Covered	
	Number	Percent	Number	Percent	Number	Percent
Public Services	(57)	(50.0)	(387)	(63.9)	(1,150,499)	(73.7)
Operating Facilities	18	15.8	83	13.7	954,565	61.2
Processing Activities	39	34.2	304	50.2	195,934	12.5
Internal Support Services	(41)	(36.0)	(143)	(23.7)	(288,421)	(18.5)
Management	15	13.2	69	11.4	39,633	2.5
Procurement/Supply	16	14.0	53	8.8	157,307	10.1
Maintenance	10	8.8	21	3.5	91,481	5.9
Industrial Activities	(16)	(14.0)	(75)	(12.4)	(121,673)	(7.8)
Major Overhaul/Repair	5	4.4	39	6.4	102,669	6.6
Manufacturing	11	9.6	36	6.0	19,004	1.2
Grand Total	114	100.0	605	100.0	1,560,593	100.0

Source: Joint Office of Management and Budget, Civil Service Commission, General Accounting Office Project, *Federal Productivity: Methods, Measurements, Results; A Staff Study to Determine the Feasibility of Developing Productivity Indices for the Federal Sector* (Washington, D.C.: U.S. Government Printing Office, 1972), p. 14.

dominant in terms of man-hours covered, accounting for about 75 percent of the entire man-years included in this subfunction. Health services were also included in this subfunction. These services accounted for about 21 percent of the total man-years covered by this subfunction. For these services, productivity increased by only 1.2 percent over the 1967-71 period. The authors of the study suggested that such results underscore "the need for a combined vigorous search for labor-saving break-throughs in these institutions."[43]

Industrial activities had the largest productivity gain during the period, increasing by 21.8 percent at an average annual rate of 5.4 percent. Within this category, manufacturing had the largest increase with productivity rising by 28.8 percent at an average annual rate of 6.5 percent. Much of this gain was attributed to the use of new capital equipment and more efficient manufacturing techniques. Although this result is interesting, it should be noted that only about 1.2 percent of the total man-years covered in the sample were included in this subfunction.

To gain a better insight into the public services function, it was divided into six segments: (1) protection of public property or public interest; (2) administration of public insurance programs; (3) assistance to the public through grants,

Table 4-5
Productivity by Function and Subfunction

	Fiscal Year					Average Annual Rate of Change (Percentage)
	1967	1968	1969	1970	1971	
Public Services	100.0	100.1	101.7	103.6	105.1	1.3
Operating Facilities	100.0	100.2	100.9	102.0	103.4	2.8
Processing Activities	100.0	100.1	106.1	112.7	115.3	3.6
Support Services	100.0	102.9	100.5	107.6	113.6	3.2
Management	100.0	101.9	91.3	112.6	105.4	1.3
Procurement and Supply	100.0	106.0	106.1	105.7	104.5	1.1
Maintenance	100.0	98.0	97.5	106.8	127.8	6.3
Industrial Activity	100.0	101.1	119.0	118.8	123.3	5.4
Major Overhaul/Repair	100.0	98.4	122.2	120.3	121.8	5.1
Manufacturing	100.0	105.8	110.8	113.9	128.8	6.5

Source: Joint Office of Management and Budget, Civil Service Commission, General Accounting Office Project, *Federal Productivity: Methods, Measurements, Results; A Staff Study to Determine the Feasibility of Developing Productivity Indices for the Federal Sector* (Washington, D.C.: U.S. Government Printing Office, 1972), pp. 193-201.

loans, applications, and documents; (4) conservation, education, and recreation services; (5) health services; and (6) information for public safety or benefit. The Postal Service was excluded from this analysis.[44] The published study does not define these categories to any extent nor does it reveal the organizations or output measures included in each.

Table 4-6 shows the change in output per unit of input for each of these six subcategories and the average annual rate of change in each. The rates of change in output per unit of input ranged from a high of 4.2 percent for protection to a low of −0.9 for information services. The authors of the study feel that the low rates of change in the latter three categories were probably the result of inadequate output measures that failed to take quality changes into account, and therefore underestimated output increases rather than reflecting an actual decline in productivity. For example, in the discussion of health services, it is argued that, "although the quality of health care has certainly improved as a result of inroads in kidney dialysis, open-heart surgery, psychotherapy, and other techniques or processes, the output measures failed to capture the full impact of these medical advances."[45]

The year-to-year variations in output per unit of input exhibited in both Tables 4-5 and 4-6 are worth noting. In some instances, these fluctuations were as great as 21.3 percent, indicating much greater irregularity in the underlying

Table 4-6
Public Service Sector by Segment

| Public Service | Fiscal Year | | | | | Average Annual Rate of Change (Percentage) |
	1967	1968	1969	1970	1971	
Protection	100.0	98.0	109.6	115.8	117.7	4.2
Public Insurance	100.0	101.0	105.7	111.6	117.2	4.0
Public Assistance	100.0	99.3	105.4	111.9	111.9	2.9
Education, Recreation	100.0	105.0	105.6	105.0	101.2	0.3
Health Services	100.0	105.0	105.6	105.0	101.2	0.3
Information Services	100.0	94.6	102.2	100.7	96.4	−0.9

Source: Joint Office of Management and Budget, Civil Service Commission, General Accounting Office Project, *Federal Productivity: Methods, Measurements, Results; A Staff Study to Determine the Feasibility of Developing Productivity Indices for the Federal Sector* (Washington, D.C.: U.S. Government Printing Office, 1972) pp. 193-201.

series. In order to better explain these fluctuations, the team requested additional information from each organizational element for any annual change greater than 5 percent. Although some of the explanations of increases of more than 5 percent centered on the more extensive use of data-processing equipment, many of the organizations attributed the increases to the employment freeze and restricted hiring practices in force during much of the period covered. Explanations of decreases of greater than 5 percent ranged from external factors beyond the control of the organization—such as the Vietnam phasedown—to changes in physical conditions at the place of work or quality improvements in output.[46]

Based on the information developed in this study, the team concluded that the rate of growth of productivity would slow down in defense-related activities because of a reduction in workload accompanied by a smaller reduction in manpower, while that of both the Postal Service and the other civilian agencies would increase because of an increase in workload with a smaller increase in manpower. On the whole they felt that the indexes for fiscal 1972 would grow at a slower rate than the 1967-71 average. Because of the work done in this study, the team felt that productivity indexes could and should be developed to cover 55 to 60 percent of total civilian federal employees and that these indexes should be centrally collected and published on a yearly basis. The need for improving measures of change in the quality of output and for including capital input was recognized, but it was not felt that these factors imposed serious limits on what could currently be done.[47]

These two reports have generated some discussion of productivity in general and government productivity in particular, but to date no additional estimates of federal government productivity have been published. Much of the discussion has been on a general level concerning the measurement of productivity and its value,[48] and some has simply been a dissemination of the findings of this most recent study.[49] The more skeptical have tended to view these reports with caution emphasizing two facts: (1) productivity is only one type of measure and should be used only in conjunction with other types of measures; and (2) expectations for what measuring productivity can do for government efficiency should not be raised too high.[50] Interestingly enough, none of this discussion has criticized the methodology used to measure federal government productivity nor the conclusions drawn from the studies.

Improving Studies of Federal
Government Productivity

As this review of the literature has suggested, studies of federal government productivity have been relatively unsophisticated as compared with the work that has been done in the private sector. The methodology used in all of the studies has been generally the same. There has been little attempt to incorporate some of the more refined techniques now quite commonly used in measuring private sector productivity. Nevertheless, these studies do represent first efforts toward solving very complex problems. And when one appreciates the complexity of these problems, these studies can be viewed as monumental efforts. Methodological criticisms and suggestions for improvement must be viewed in this context.

Sample Selection. All of the studies of federal government productivity have been quite limited in their man-year coverage. The most ambitious, the 1972 study, covered only about 56 percent of the total civilian federal government employee man-years. None of the studies included military man-years. Yet in 1971 the military service had 2,519,000 persons on active duty as compared to 2,766,000 civilian full-time employees of the federal government.[51] The exclusion of military employees omits almost half of the total federal work force as well as about 37 percent of the total federal budget. Thus the study actually covers only about 28 percent of total federal employment, not 56 percent. The findings should, therefore, not be interpreted as an index of aggregate federal government productivity.

Those agencies tending to have greatest contact with the citizen-taxpayer had rather limited coverage. For HEW and HUD, the study covered only about 58 percent and 56 percent respectively of those agencies' total man-years. For DOT the sample coverage dropped to about 30 percent and for Agriculture only about 28 percent of the total man-years were included in the study. The Social Security Administration was the primary HEW element included. The only part of HUD covered by the study was FHA, while for DOT only some parts of the FAA and the Coast Guard were included. Agriculture placed fourteen elements in the study, but of this group of departments, Agriculture had the lowest total percentage coverage. Total man-hour coverage was obtained only for the Postal Service, now a government enterprise, the SEC, and the NLRB, both regulatory agencies. This kind of coverage can hardly be considered a random sampling. One is left with the problem of how to interpret the aggregate index. What does a productivity index based on this sample actually measure? What do the results mean? Can inferences for all of HUD's activities, for example, be drawn from the operation of FHA?

The study team did construct two additional indexes, one weighted by the actual distribution of federal employees and one weighted by the actual distribution of employees in different pay systems, to correct for the bias in the sample. These changes did not make a great difference in terms of results. For the original sample, productivity grew at an average annual rate of 1.9 percent, whereas for the sample weighted by actual employment segments it grew at 2.1 percent. When weighted by major pay systems, it grew at an average annual rate of 2.3 percent.

These two indexes do provide additional insight into federal government productivity growth, but they do not correct the sample to reflect the distribution of employees among activities within each of the agencies involved.

The study team also constructed public service subfunction indexes, covering such things as health services, public assistance, and so forth. These indexes are based on the original sample. The study team did not provide information on the percentage of total employees engaged in each subfunction covered by the sample. Does the index of health services cover 1 percent of all those employees concerned with the provision of health services or does it cover 98 percent of all such employees? Without this information it is impossible to determine how representative this index is or what inferences can be drawn from it.

There is a second problem with this sample—the percentage of employees covered is only one method of determining its relevance. An alternative method would be to determine the percentage of total labor cost covered by the sample. Labor cost information was requested from each of the participating agencies, but it was not published in the final report. A third method for determining the importance of the sample, probably more important from the viewpoint of the citizen-taxpayer, is the percentage of total federal expenditures sampled, as an indication of the quantity of total resources employed.

The primary reason suggested for the lack of population coverage was the difficulties involved in measuring outputs. Obviously more work needs to be done in this area, but it is premature to describe an index based on this sample as an aggregate index of federal government productivity. At this point in the "state of the art" separate productivity indexes for individual departments and agencies should be emphasized. Publishing individual indexes might cause some political problems, as the study team suggested, but individual indexes would have been much more reliable indicators of productivity changes.

Output Measures. Traditionally one of the primary reasons for scepticism surrounding studies of federal productivity has centered on the estimates of output. Reading the list of output measures used in the most recent study leaves one with the nagging suspicion that everything which could be counted was used as an output measure. Since output measures did have to meet certain criteria, one must assume that such a suspicion is incorrect. Yet some exceptionally weak output indicators are included in this study. For example, for the Department of Interior, Bureau of Indian Affairs, one element is direct education. BIA operates Indian boarding schools, day schools, and dormitories. The output of this program is measured by the number of students enrolled. Another element is public school education. Its purpose is to provide assistance to public schools. The output measure is the number of Indian students enrolled in public schools.[52]

The number of students enrolled is not a reliable measure of the output of programs designed to provide education for Indians. According to this measure, if the number of students increases while educational personnel remains constant, educational productivity increases. Better measures of educational output have been suggested and could be applied.

In addition to the fact that some of the output measures are weak, two other problems haunt the output indicators used in this study. First, insufficient attention has been paid to what exactly is supposed to be measured. For many of the federal agencies, the goal is to measure the quantity of services performed by those agencies. To illustrate, consider different types of federal insurance, a number of which were included in this study. In most cases, the output measure used was the number of transactions weighted by the proportion of labor time required for each transaction. The implicit assumption is that the quantity of service rendered is proportional to the number of transactions weighted by the relative labor time required for each transaction.

Compare this assumption to that made when estimating the quantity of services provided by private sector retail stores. There the assumption is that the quantity of service was proportional to the dollar value of each transaction, not the number of transactions. The quantity of service of federal insurance agencies may be proportional to the number of transactions, as this method implies. If it is, then possibly the method used to estimate service by retail stores should be changed. In any case, this assumption deserves some discussion and justification for its use, but none was provided.

Included within this problem is the question of when a service is provided. Again using federal insurance programs as an example, the general procedure was to count the number of applications for acceptance into the program, the number of applications processed, the number of claims processed, and the number of claim payments made, each as a separate output. The question is whether or not a quantity of service is provided at each step in this process as this method of counting outputs assumes. It may be argued that from the point of view of the person insured, only at the time a claim is paid is any service actually provided. All of the steps leading up to the payment of the claim may be considered intermediate and not final output. In this view, all of those steps are work measures, but not output measures. Again what is needed is some justification for the method actually used and some discussion of where the service is provided. Without such a discussion, the reader is left with the justifiable impression that the output of a number of services has been double-counted.

The second general problem is that of final versus intermediate output measures. The 1972 study includes intermediate outputs. It justifies this by defining productivity as "how well does one (or all) Federal employee(s) perform work."[53] Intermediate products can be included as long as they are "mutually exclusive." Such an interpretation confuses work and productivity measures. In productivity measurement the interest is in measuring the efficiency of producing final products, not in the intermediate stages of production. Using both intermediate and final products and then aggregating them into one index double-counts the actual quantity of services and therefore overestimates output quantities. This is true even if intermediate products are mutually exclusive.

All of these studies of federal government productivity use the direct output method for estimating the quantity of government output. More discrimination in the selection of output measures and more consideration of the point in the production process where a service is actually provided would reduce the number of output measures and improve the overall quality of the study; confidence in the results would be increased.

Weighting. The studies of federal government productivity have weighted output estimates by the proportion of labor time necessary to provide that output. The BOB's 1964 study developed two additional indexes, one using constant-dollar payroll cost weights and the other using constant-dollar total cost weights. The 1972 study also tried two other types of weighting techniques, one using the relative proportion of labor time based on the distribution of labor among the agencies and one weighting by the distribution of labor within different pay categories. In neither the BOB study nor the 1972 study did the alternate weighting procedures make a significant difference in the results.

Weights have two purposes. First, multiplying heterogeneous units of output by a common weighting unit yields a unit of measure that can be added. Any item common to all of the heterogeneous output units will serve this purpose. Second, weights reflect the relative importance of different outputs. For example, in the private sector, prices are often used as weights. A good selling for $2 receives twice the weight of a good selling for $1. Using labor-time weights in the public sector is one method for determining the relative importance of different outputs. It estimates the relative importance of different types of output from the point of view of the production process—the proportion of labor time required to produce that output as compared to other outputs.

There are other methods of estimating relative importance. One alternative approach would be to weight by the proportion of total expenditures associated with the provision of each particular output. Such a weighting system may be of greater interest to the citizen-taxpayer because it would reflect the importance of each output in terms of the total proportion of taxpayer's resources used to provide that output. This kind of a weighting procedure was approached in the 1964 BOB study but has not been tried in other studies of federal government productivity. Further experimentation with this approach would appear to be useful.

Inputs. The major problem in the estimates of inputs for all of the federal studies is the absence of a capital input. Without estimates of capital flows, measuring total factor productivity is impossible and the effects of factor substitution cannot be determined. This deficiency has been recognized in a number of the studies of federal government productivity, but as yet no method for including capital has been developed.

The federal studies could also be improved by including estimated changes in the quality of labor. Either Denison's or Kendrick's methods could be employed. The information is available and by so doing the reliability of these indexes could be improved.

Interpretation of Results. A fifth comment on the studies of federal government productivity, particularly the 1972 study, centers on the way in which the results are interpreted and conclusions are drawn. When discussing future trends in federal government productivity, the authors of the 1972 study suggest that productivity in Defense will have a downward trend in fiscal 1972 and 1973 because workload (output) will fall while employment will fall at a less rapid rate. Productivity in the Postal Service will continue to grow because there will be a growth in workload with little growth in employment, while productivity in other civilian agencies will grow because there will be a growth of workload with little or no growth in employment.[54] In the latter two cases, the authors are saying that the numerator of the productivity ratio will grow faster than the denominator. Obviously if this happens, productivity—by definition—will increase. The question that must be asked is why? What factors have been important in the growth in federal productivity in the past? What factors will encourage this predicted future growth?

In the 1972 study there is occasionally an interpretation of results, as in the differential productivity in the wage board category as compared with the general pay schedule category.[55] More of such analysis would be useful. A productivity study is more than simply a problem of index numbers. The purpose of such a study is not only to identify where productivity has increased, but also and more importantly why it has increased, and whether experience can be transferred to other areas. Measurement without analysis is not always useful.

Quality. The major deficiency with the studies of federal government productivity is the lack of attention to changes in the quality of outputs. None of the studies have incorporated quality changes into output estimates, implying that over the period of the particular study the quality of federal government services has not changed. Such a position is difficult to accept. Ignoring quality leaves the analyst (and the reader) in the rather awkward position of having no idea of exactly what is measured.

Perspectives

The general methodology used in federal productivity studies has changed remarkably little over the forty-year period since the Bowden research on the Postal Service in 1932. All of the studies use the direct output method for estimating changes in federal government productivity. All use some variant of man-hours as the only input factor, and all weight by the proportion of man-hours required to produce each output. Yet when one considers the context of these efforts, the difficulties that must be faced in measuring federal government output, one realizes that these studies do constitute a major first step toward estimating productivity in the public sector. This whole body of work does demonstrate that reasonable estimates of federal government productivity, particularly at the agency level, can be developed.

Local Government Productivity

The fiscal pressures faced by the local public sector have been generated most recently by increasing service costs, more militant public employees unions, and the "taxpayers' revolt" of the late 1960s and early 1970s. Local government efficiency has become a popular topic. Although most of the journalism on this subject has been directed at the as-yet unfulfilled promises of the National Commission on Productivity—promises of developing ways to measure and increase local government productivity—some reporters have dealt with the problems of productivity measurement and the ways in which certain cities, primarily New York City, were trying to improve productivity.[56] The degree of concern over local government efficiency is heightened when one realizes that the principal fact which can be stated is that little is known.

As compared to the work done on local government productivity, federal efforts appear to be a mature area of endeavor. The obstacles imposed by inadequate estimates of public output loom even larger at the local level than at the national level. There is very little information available on the direct outputs of local governments. Most local governments simply do not keep the data necessary to measure such outputs, and those that do have only recently begun to keep the data on a systematic basis. An Urban Institute survey of thirty cities and counties found that only about half of those surveyed collected cost data by activity and program on a routine basis; about three-fourths collected workload information; slightly less than one-third collected data on cost per unit workload; and only four—Chicago, Dade County, Dayton, and Los Angeles— regularly collected effectiveness or impact data.[57] Even in those few juris- dictions where the necessary data are available, because of the fragmentation of local governments and differing patterns in the assignment of responsibilities, much of it is not comparable among jurisdictions.

As a result, the search for local government output surrogates continues, with controversy over what is to be measured—direct outputs or consequences. The empirical studies of federal government productivity suggest that at least a tacit agreement has been reached on measurement methods. In the area of local government productivity, no such agreement has been reached. These problems are compounded by the lack of attention that professional economists have given to the subject.

Background

One of the first systematic inquiries into techniques for measuring local government output was authored by Clarence E. Ridley and Herbert A. Simon in 1938.[58] They suggested possible output measures for fire, police, public education, public libraries, personnel, municipal finance, and city planning. As an example, in the case of fire protection, five possible measures were suggested: expenditures, standards of effort, distribution of equipment, fire and fire loss rates, and fire and fire loss rates by type of property.[59] In the course of their discussion of measurement techniques, the concept of efficiency is stressed, but it is defined in terms of consequences rather than direct outputs.

The efficiency of administration is measured by the ratio of the effects actually obtained with the available resources to the maximum effects possible with the available resources.[60]

In other words, "efficiency is a relationship between an effect and the resources that produce it."[61]

This emphasis on consequences was carried over into the area of planning-pro- gramming-budgeting systems, culminating in the PPBS emphasis on evaluation at both the national and local level. In the process the entire area of efficiency in terms of the relationship of inputs and direct outputs was left almost completely untouched.

In 1960 Henry J. Schmandt and G. Ross Stephens moved toward a direct output approach by using a rather novel method for measuring local government output.[62] They developed a service level index for the nineteen cities and villages within Milwaukee County. To obtain service levels, each municipal function was broken down into its subfunctions or activities. The *service level* was defined as simply the number of different activities performed for each function. Police protection, for example, was divided into 65 different categories; 550 different municipal subfunctions were identified for this study. Schmandt and Stephens found that the number of subfunctions provided by each municipality was highly correlated with population, age of the municipality, and total expenditures. Based on these findings, they suggested that their service-level index was a good measure of municipal output.

Whether or not such an index provides reasonable estimates of municipal output is questionable, but not really of great concern for present inquiry. The importance of the study lies in the fact that it returns to the concept of direct output rather than effect as the proper unit for the analysis of local government productivity.

Although not referring specifically to local government, in 1964 Bertram M. Gross suggested four possible surrogates that could be used to estimate the quantity of intangible services. These included the number of clients, the duration of the service, the intermediate or subsequent products of the service, and finally our old friend, service input factors.[63] Gross' intermediate or subsequent product surrogate is basically a direct output measure. Thus Gross suggests that direct output may be a reliable quantity measure of intangible services, i.e., local government services.

Bradford, Malt, and Oates' Study

Although a number of empirical studies estimating the shape of the cost function for certain local government services have been attempted,[64] only one empirical study relevant to local government productivity measurement has been completed to date. In an attempt to evaluate the Baumol "disease" hypothesis, Bradford, Malt, and Oates examined the increase in the cost of D-output for education, health and hospitals, police, fire, and public welfare.[65] Table 4-7 summarizes their findings.

Current educational cost per pupil day increased at an annual rate of 6.7 percent over the postwar period. Over the same period, the average annual salaries of city public school teachers increased at an annual rate of 4.8 percent, whereas the wholesale price index increased by only 1.4 percent per year. Thus the bundle of goods in terms of wholesale prices that must be given up for a

Table 4-7
The Cost of Local Government Services

		Annual Rate of Increase (Compounded Percentage)
Education–Current Cost per Pupil Day		
	1900-1967	5.0
	1947-1967	6.7
Health and Hospitals–Hospital Daily Service Charge		
	1935-1963	6.5
	1947-1963	7.4
State and Local Government Short-Term and Other Special Hospitals–Average Total Expenses per Patient Day		
	1946-1965	9.6
Police–Per Capita Expenditures		
	1902-1966	4.7
	1946-1966	7.1
Fire–Per Capita Expenditures		
	1902-1966	4.2
	1946-1966	6.2
Public Welfare		(No estimates provided)

Source: Summarized from D.F. Bradford, R.A. Malt, and W.E. Oates, "The Rising Cost of Local Government Services: Some Evidence and Reflections," *National Tax Journal* 22 (June 1969): 185-202.

pupil-day of education increased by about 5.3 percent per year.[b]

Bradford, Malt, and Oates recognized that the quality of education has improved but doubted that the rate of increase was comparable with the increase in cost. Rather they suggested that rising relative unit costs of education resulted from little technological change and therefore low rates of productivity growth. They argue:

---

[b]The authors do discuss other reasons for the rapid increase in educational costs. For example, because of lack of incentives, the public education system may simply be inefficient, or powerful interest groups, primarily the professional educators, may block the use of technological innovations. More interestingly, they suggest that a part of the relative increase in cost may be the result of a movement along the production possibilities frontier. Assume we plot such a frontier with education on one axis and all other goods on the other axis. If we assume that the frontier is linear, the concern of Baumol's hypothesis is with a shift in the all other goods intercept away from the origin with no such shift of the educational intercept. The result would be an increase in the slope of the frontier and therefore an increasing opportunity cost for education. If on the other hand, we assume a frontier concave to the origin, a simple transfer of resources from all other goods to education will increase the relative opportunity cost of additional education. The authors do not seem to feel that this kind of a movement along the production-possibilities frontier could be the major reason for the rapid increase in educational cost.

it seems to us unlikely, however, that the technology by which a teacher produces a "geography-lesson-equivalent" has advanced at a rate comparable to the rate of increase of teacher compensation, or that the "geography-lesson-equivalents" transmitted to a student have increased at a rate comparable to expenditure per-student.[66]

In their examination of health and hospitals, Bradford, Malt, and Oates found that the hospital daily service charge had increased at an annual rate of 7.4 percent over the postwar period, while the average total expenses per patient day for state and local government short-term and other special hospitals increased at a yearly rate of 9.6 percent for the period 1946-65. Again the authors recognized that the quality of hospital services has increased and that major technological improvements have occurred, but they contend that most of these improvements have not been of a cost-saving nature. They believe that the major reason for increasing costs in this area is lagging productivity.

Per capita local government expenditures on police and fire increased at an annual rate of 7.1 and 6.2 percent respectively during the postwar period. In an attempt to determine whether this increase represented an increase in the output of these services or was simply the result of rising unit cost, the authors "deflated" the increase in expenditures by the increase in police employment and fire protection employment for the period 1952 to 1963 for cities of over 50,000. Police employment increased from 20.6 to 23.9 per 10,000 population, while fire protection employment increased from 14.8 to 16.3 per 10,000 population from 1952 to 1963. Deflating for this increase in police per person and firemen per person reduced the annual rate of increase from 6.1 percent to 4.7 for police and from 4.8 percent to 4.0 percent for fire. The authors did not seem to feel that these changes were particularly significant and suggested that the primary reason for the increase in both police and fire expenditure was rising unit costs.

Although the authors also examined the public welfare function, they reached no conclusion regarding the increase of unit cost for this function. As a matter of fact, realizing that much of this function consists of making direct transfer payments, they found it difficult to even make sense out of the unit cost concept. The authors do think that one-shot gains in productivity could be obtained by improving the efficiency of welfare record-keeping; they do not provide any evidence on historic changes in productivity for this function.

Bradford, Malt, and Oates conclude that the primary reason for the increases in local government budgets is rising unit costs. They feel that the technological improvements made have not been of a cost-reducing nature. They conclude by saying that

the historical record together with some further reflections indicate to us that local (especially large city) governments can probably expect that costs will continue to rise cumulatively and at a more rapid rate than those in the rest of the economy even if there is no increase either in the quantity or quality of the services provided.[67]

Thus they suggest that the evidence supports Baumol's hypothesis.

Bradford, Malt, and Oates' study is the first empirical investigation of aggregate local government productivity. Since it is the first, they did rely heavily on speculation. To make their case, they need additional evidence of changes in both the quantity and quality of output. Yet their study does provide hope for future empirical investigation into local government productivity at an aggregate level. They do make some refinements; for example, they adjust for changes in the quality of education, police, and fire by taking into account changes in the teacher-pupil ratio and changes in the number of police and firemen per capita. Their study does point toward a new and promising direction.

The Urban Institute Study

In conjunction with the work of the National Commission on Productivity, the Urban Institute undertook a four-part study of local government productivity in 1971. Part I of the study is a summary of the findings of the other three parts. Part II concentrates on developing productivity measurements for solid waste collection, while part III suggests ways in which the productivity of police crime control may be measured. Naturally, the basic goals of these two parts of the study were to improve productivity measurement in solid waste collection and police crime control respectively. Part IV deals with the development of procedures for identifying and evaluating innovations which may be used to improve productivity within local governments.[68]

After examining the problems surrounding local government productivity measurement, the reasons for such measurement, and the current state of the art, the Institute developed a number of recommendations for both measuring and improving local government productivity. Their principal recommendation was for a two- or three-year study and analysis of local government productivity to be jointly sponsored by the federal government and by local government associations.

In their discussion of local government productivity measurement, the Institute argued that output should be broadly defined, contending that "the 'volume of products or services produced' is [should be] interpreted in the broad sense to include the ideas of effectiveness and quality, not merely efficiency and quantity."[69] The emphasis on quality and effectiveness was stressed through these studies and the Institute continued to point out that:

Productivity should not be estimated in such a way as to ignore the 'quality' of the product or service, particularly in relation to the effects or impacts on the citizens and the community. We believe productivity estimates based on a narrow definition of output to mean solely the immediate products such as 'tons of garbage collected', 'gallons of sewage treated', 'number of examinations given', can be uninformative and even grossly misleading.[70]

Note the contrast between this position and that of Bradford, Malt, and Oates. The position of the Institute seems to be that Bradford, Malt, and Oates' distinction between C and D-output is at best artificial when applied to measuring local government productivity. At worst, it is "grossly misleading." To be useful and not misleading, the Institute suggests that both efficiency and effectiveness measures of output must be employed. The implication of this reasoning is that one should not search for a single measure of local government productivity. Rather, multiple measures of productivity for each local government function should be developed. In parts II and III of the study, multiple productivity measures of both solid waste collection and police crime control are suggested. Table 4-8 shows the suggested measures for police crime control. Thirteen separate measures are identified; current information is available for five of the measures. Additional data would have to be collected for the other eight measures. Almost all of these measures estimate changes in either the effectiveness of the service or the quality of the service.

The Institute suggests an interesting method for estimating parts of the

Table 4-8

Productivity Measurements for the Police Crime Control Function[a]

A. *Currently Available*

   1. Population served per police employee and per dollar[b]

   2. Crime rate and changes in crime rates for reported crimes (relative to dollars or employees per capita)

   3. Clearance rates of reported crimes (relative to dollars or employees per capita)

   4. Arrests per police department employee and per dollar[b]

   5. Clearances per police department employee and per dollar[b]

B. *Requiring Significant Additional Data Gathering*

   1. Crime rates including estimates of unreported crimes based on victimization studies

   2. Clearance rates based on estimates of unreported victimization studies

   3. Percent of felony arrests that "survive" preliminary hearings in courts of limited jurisdiction

   4. Percent of arrests that lead to convictions

   5. Average response times for calls for service

   6. Percent of crimes solved in less than X days

   7. Percent of population indicating a lack of feeling of security

   8. Percent of population expressing dissatisfaction with police services

[a]These (except for A-1, B-7 and B-8) should be disaggregated by type of crime, with emphasis on the most "important" crime.

[b]Data on resource inputs should to the extent possible exclude resources expended on noncrime control functions such as traffic control.

Source: The Urban Institute, *The Challenge of Productivity Diversity: Part III, Measuring Police-Crime Control Productivity*, Prepared for the National Commission on Productivity (Washington, D.C.: Urban Institute, 1972), p. 10.

productivity of solid waste collection. The suggested output measure is tons of solid waste collected, adjusted for changes in quality. Two factors are used to reflect changes in the quality of the service: an average street cleanliness rating where the rating is based on a scale of 1 to 4, and the percentage of population expressing satisfaction with solid waste collection based on a survey. The output estimate is the tons of solid waste collected, multiplied by the cleanliness rating and the percentage of persons satisfied with collection, yielding a quantity measure, adjusted for changes in quality. A base year is chosen and an output index is developed. The input measure is real dollar costs. Again an index is developed using the same base year. Dividing the output index by the input index yields an index of productivity.[71]

The significant part of this example is the quality adjustment procedure. As long as people are more satisfied with cleaner streets, these two quality indicators should be highly correlated. The average street cleanliness rating measures the relative effect of the service, the cleanliness of a street either over time or in comparison with other streets. The survey measures at least two things, the quality or the effect of the service (assuming that persons are more satisfied with cleaner streets) and the quality of the delivery of the service (assuming that people are more satisfied the less noisy the collection, and so forth). How much weight is given to effect in the survey as opposed to delivery depends upon the specific questions asked and the weights given to each answer. In any case, this overall quality adjustment procedure weights changes in effect more heavily than changes in the quality of delivery. Any change in effect will be counted both by the cleanliness rating and the survey, whereas any change in the quality of delivery will only be counted once, in the survey. The result is that certain types of quality changes are double-counted whereas others are not.

There is a second interesting point about this particular quality adjustment. The cleanliness rating is a quality change from the perspective of the analyst. The survey measures quality from the perspective of the population served. Under this method, both views of quality change are given equal weight. It may be worthwhile to include both points of view, but should they be given equal weights in the weighting system? Or how should the value of the different points of view be divided?

Part III of the Urban Institute's study examines police crime-control productivity. After identifying the thirteen productivity measurements listed in Table 4-8, the Institute uses traditional determinants analysis in an attempt to group cities for productivity study and to identify factors which may explain variations in productivity. By relating certain of their productivity measures to both population and socioeconomic characteristics, they find wide unexplained variations in performance among cities, suggesting large differences in police productivity.

To determine national trends in police productivity, the Institute examined the percentage changes in eight of their productivity measures for the years

1965-70. Table 4-9 shows their results. Although the Institute was quite hesitant to draw conclusions from this table, they did say that the increase in both the number of police per 100,000 population and indexed crime per 100,000 implied a fall in productivity. Actually, every measure contained in this table implies a decline in the productivity of police crime control.[72]

This study by the Urban Institute is an excellent explanation of the problems surrounding local government productivity measurement. The future directions suggested by the study seem to be much less useful. In general the Institute suggested that outputs be measured by the consequences method and that productivity be defined as the ratio of effects to inputs. This approach lacks a strong theoretical base. It ignores the intermediate step, that of direct outputs. A

Table 4-9
National Averages and Trends for Selected Productivity Measurements[a,b]

	Cities over 250,000		Cities 100-250,000	
	1970	Percentage Change from 1965 to 1970	1970	Percentage Change from 1965 to 1970
Reported Index Crimes per 100,000	5,340	+117	4,280	+100
Police per 100,000	326	+ 23	204	+ 24
Index Crimes per Police employee[c]	16.4	+ 76	21.0	+ 67
Index Crime Clearances per Police Employee[c]	3.6	+ 44	3.9	+ 23
Clearance Rate	0.218	− 20	0.188	− 25
Proportion of Crimes in Lowest Clearance Rate Categories[d]	0.45	− 4	0.49	+ 11
Clearance Rate for Lowest Clearance Rate Categories[d]	0.149	− 53	0.122	− 60
Total Expenditures per Police Employee, Current Dollars[e]	$14,500	+ 11	$12,100	+ 7

[a]Sources of data: FBI Crimes in the United States, Uniform Crime Reports; and ICMA Municipal Yearbook.

[b]All averages are unweighted, e.g., total crimes summed over all cities divided by total police employees summed over all cities.

[c]The number of police employees was the average number for the year.

[d]Defined here as larcenies and auto thefts.

[e]The number of police employees in the middle of fiscal year (end of calendar year).

Source: The Urban Institute, *The Challenge of Productivity Diversity: Part III, Measuring Police-Crime Control Productivity*, Prepared for the National Commission on Productivity (Washington, D.C.: Urban Institute, 1972), p. 67.

great deal can be learned from an analysis of this intermediate step. The method suggested by the Urban Institute is most useful for program evaluation. It holds less promise as a method for measuring local government productivity.

The New York City Approach

Even though local government productivity has not as yet been successfully measured, the mounting pressures of increasing costs have forced some local governments to develop ways of improving productivity. New York City is far ahead in this area.

Under the pressures of increasing wage demands, the City began a productivity program. As a part of this program, the City demanded that any wage increase above a cost-of-living increase be supported by measurable improvements in productivity. The City has experienced most success in those areas where there is a clearly definable measure of output. For example, in the area of rat control, by rescheduling inspections and introducing tight time and performance standards, the City was able to reduce the cost per inspection from $9.10 to $2.74 and the cost per extermination from $22.50 to $4.98. In the area of sanitation vehicle maintenance, by establishing vehicle maintenance districts and improving the parts delivery system, the garage time for trucks was reduced from 38 percent to 18 percent.

In those areas where outputs are harder to define, the City has concentrated on improving the deployment of resources. For example, in the area of police dispatching a new computer system called the Special Police Radio Inquiry Network has made it possible for city police to respond to 95 percent of all calls in thirty seconds or less.

Even the introduction of some fairly simple management techniques has proved most effective in the reduction of both time and cost. The development of a Capital Construction Information System, which requires monthly progress reports on capital construction and clearly defines lines of responsibility, has been instrumental in reducing the time required for the planning and construction of new buildings by one-half.[73]

New York City has taken a highly operational approach to local government productivity. By ignoring consequences and concentrating on direct outputs and manpower deployment, they have been able to tie productivity measurement to collective bargaining agreements, forcing the whole issue into the realm of labor-management relations. In the process they have made both sides much more aware of what can be done to improve the efficiency of public service delivery. The results of New York City's efforts are impressive. Note that this approach is different from that of the federal government and from the other "academic" studies that have been reviewed in this chapter. Combining these two approaches should certainly bring increased insight into the whole spectrum of local government productivity.

Other Approaches

There have been some other attempts to improve local government productivity. In their study, the Urban Institute identified six productivity-improving innovations which they felt would be of interest to other local governments. These were: the one-man, nonmechanized refuse collection system used in Inglewood, California; the one-man, mechanized collection system used in Bellaire, Texas, and Scottsdale, Arizona; the computer-assisted, solid waste collection system used in Wichita Falls, Texas, and Baton Rouge, Louisiana; the Dallas police department's use of helicopters; and the manpower resource allocation model used in the Kansas City, Missouri, police department. In only the first two cases did the Urban Institute find substantial cost reductions from these innovations. The other innovations had advantages such as increasing the number of minority employees or reducing crime, but not at a reduction in cost.[74]

Other units of government have also demonstrated an interest in improving productivity. For example, the governor of Wisconsin recently established a productivity improvement target of 2.5 percent per year.[75] Los Angeles County adopted a system of social service contracts in their welfare department which they feel will improve the efficiency of that department.[76]

Many of these innovations do have the potential for providing substantial cost savings to local governments. Even more important than these potential savings is the commitment on the part of these local governments to improving the efficiency of service provision. Relying on this commitment and on the present level of technology, it is possible to hope for a substantial increase in local government productivity.

Summary

This chapter examined in some detail the empirical studies of federal and local government productivity. A number of advances have been made in estimating federal government productivity. Although research has not yet reached the point of providing a reliable aggregate index of federal government productivity, estimates of federal government productivity have come a long way. If the research continues, it should be possible, in a reasonably short period of time, to build a reliable index of federal government productivity by agency, even if a reliable aggregate index remains elusive.

The two major empirical local government studies are the Bradford, Malt, and

Oates' research and the Urban Institute's study. These two disagreed on method; Bradford, Malt, and Oates emphasized the distinction between C and D-outputs, and the Urban Institute suggests that output be measured in terms of consequences.

Chapter 5 suggests an additional method for measuring local government productivity, a method which requires less information, and which is promising in terms of operational application.

5 Measuring Changes in Local Government Expenditure*

A number of the questions asked by citizens about governmental operations are questions that cannot be answered in a straightforward way by economists. Economists may be able to serve up some approximate answers or provide some insights; case studies of governmental functions in a specific jurisdiction may be helpful, but all approaches have their limitations.

Economists cannot provide definitive answers to some legitimate citizen questions because, as previously emphasized, there is no precise way to measure government service output. The public sector does not provide a commodity output that is homogeneous over time, as is approximately the case with tons of steel of specified dimensions, or aluminum ingots or barrels of cement. Rather it provides a complex service output whose quality varies from year to year.

Other difficulties limit the kinds of answers economists can give to these questions. These difficulties include the definition of a production function for the public sector and the absence of data, particularly at the local government level.

Previous Research

Relatively little research has been devoted to the analysis of the sources of change over time in state-local or local government expenditure, in contrast with the very large body of research that has been devoted to an analysis of the socioeconomic and political determinants of expenditure at a point in time— cross-section analysis (see Chapter 3). Thus the concept of scope and quality, which is thought to be necessary for a time-series study, has not received the attention that would otherwise have been the case.

However, some attention to this concept has emerged from the work that has been done on expenditure elasticities and on state-local expenditure projections. Hirsch, for example, introduced a scope and quality index in his study of expenditure elasticity for St. Louis County schools, in his 1959 publication for the Joint Economic Committee.[1] Netzer discussed the concept briefly in an unpublished memorandum for the Committee for Economic Development in 1966 and also in a Joint Economic Committee publication.[2] The CED publication in 1967, *A Fiscal Program for a Balanced Federalism*, and a CED Supplementary Paper the following year also discussed scope and quality in the context of an analysis of changes in government expenditure.[3]

---

*The mathematical model in this chapter was developed by Polly A. Burkhead.

Selma Mushkin's projections for the Council of State Governments in 1965 did not utilize the concept extensively in the examination of particular functions, but she did examine scope and quality in summary articles.[4] In an *RES* article, Mushkin and Lupo presented a table to show, for the years 1954-64, the per annum growth in personal service expenditures for the state-local sector and the additive components of that growth defined as "workload," "cost per unit" and "quality and scope of service." In a companion article, Mushkin and Lupo defined the following relationship:[5]

$$\frac{\text{Relative Rate of Growth in State and Local}}{\text{Government Expenditures}}$$

$$\begin{pmatrix} \text{Relative Rate of Growth in} \\ \text{Workload} \end{pmatrix} \times \begin{pmatrix} \text{Relative Rate of Growth in} \\ \text{Cost per Unit} \end{pmatrix}.$$

This computation yields a residual that was described as scope and quality.[a] Mushkin and Lupo addressed the scope and quality issue by direct comparisons of public- and private-sector wage rates. They suggested that an improvement in the quality of government services could be interpreted through an improvement in the relative wages paid to government employees.

In 1969 William H. Robinson of the U.S. Bureau of the Budget made a further contribution to the analysis of state-local expenditure changes.[6] Although Robinson was primarily concerned with a review of state-local projections, he did examine the influences on state-local spending from 1962 to 1967 in terms of "population, weighted," "prices," and "scope and quality" and provided some estimates of average annual increases for a number of state-local expenditure functions.[b]

In 1971 the Brookings Institution published *Setting National Priorities: The 1972 Budget*, edited by Charles L. Schultze. The volume contained an article on revenue sharing by Robert D. Reischauer, and there is an underlying, unpublished memorandum which sets forth Reischauer's methodology.[7] His is the first effort to partition expenditure increases numerically, as a percentage contribution to each of the components of change. These estimates are reproduced here as Table 5-1.

---

[a]It may be noted that this approach is conceptually comparable with the decomposition, over time, of the revenue of a firm or industry. Between t_1 and t_2 changes in revenue can be attributed to changes in price and changes in quantity.

[b]The formula that Robinson employed is not specifically described but appears to be of the following form:

$$\frac{E_t}{E_o} = \left(\frac{P_t}{P_o}\right)\left(\frac{PR_t}{PR_o}\right)\left(\frac{S_t \ \& \ Q_t}{S_o \ \& \ Q_o}\right)$$

where o is the beginning year, t the terminal year, P is the population weighted, PR is price change, and S and Q are scope and quality.

Table 5-1
Comparison of State and Local Expenditures, by Function, Fiscal Years 1955 and 1969 (Amounts in Billions of Dollars)

Function	Amount 1955	Amount 1969	1955-69 Percentage Increase	1955-69 Percentage of Total Increase	Percentage of 1955-69 Increase in Expenditure Attributable to Increase in Workload	Percentage of 1955-69 Increase in Expenditure Attributable to Increase in Price	Percentage of 1955-69 Increase in Expenditure Attributable to Increase in Scope and Quality
All Functions	39.0	134.1	244.1	100.0	–	–	–
General Expenditure	33.7	116.7	246.1	87.2	26.2	43.8	30.0
Local Schools	10.1	33.8	233.2	24.8	31.7	52.4	15.9
Higher Education and Other Education, Except Local Schools	1.8	13.5	657.6	12.3	25.1	35.5	39.4
Public Welfare	3.2	12.1	282.2	9.4	–	29.7	70.3
Highways	6.5	15.4	138.9	9.4	50.8	42.3	6.9
Hospitals and Health	2.5	8.5	237.5	6.3	18.8	43.8	37.4
Basic Urban Services[a]	4.3	14.9	243.7	11.1	22.8	50.6	26.6
Administration and Other[b]	5.3	18.5	247.4	13.9	18.5	38.0	43.6
Utility Deficit	0.4	1.4	234.5	1.0	–	–	–
Debt Retirement and Additions to Liquid Assets[c,d]	3.9	12.0	206.1	8.5	–	–	–
Contributions to Retirement Systems	0.9	4.0	339.8	3.2	–	–	–

[a]Includes fire protection, police protection, correction, sewerage, other sanitation, parks and recreation, housing and urban renewal, and transportation and terminals.

[b]Includes administration and general control, general public buildings, interest on general debt, employment services, and miscellaneous functions.

[c]Excludes assets of social insurance funds.

[d]Estimated.

Source: Robert D. Reischauer, in Charles L. Schultze, et al., eds., *Setting National Priorities, the 1972 Budget* (Washington: Brookings Institution, 1971), p. 139, © 1971 by the Brookings Institution, Washington, D.C.

Reischauer's description of his model may be quoted directly:

The growth in Expenditures (E) is assumed to be related to the growth in Workload (W), Price (P), Scope (S), and Quality (Q) in the following manner:

$$\frac{E_t}{E_s} = \frac{W_t}{W_s} \times \frac{P_t}{P_s} \times \frac{S_t}{S_s} \times \frac{Q_t}{Q_s}$$

where subscripts s and t denote the values of the relevant index in the starting and terminal years.[8]

The price index that is employed by Reischauer varies from function to function. For local schools it is a combination of average monthly earnings of school employees, construction costs, and procurement costs. For welfare the price deflator takes into account both the salaries of welfare workers and the transfer payments to welfare recipients. There are similar variations in the price index relevant to each functional category of government expenditure.

In an attempt to refine the scope and quality concept, Reischauer introduced a different definition of workload than had hitherto been utilized. He defined *workload* as the portion of the total population available to be served by a specific governmental program (welfare, education, highways, etc.) and *scope* as the proportion of that relevant population that was, in fact, served. Thus, in education the population of school age was workload and the proportion of that school age population actually in school was designated as scope. In welfare the population below the poverty line was taken as workload, and the proportion of that population on welfare was taken as scope. In the published version of Reischauer's work, the scope and quality measures are combined in the ratio R_2/R_1, although they are kept separate in the unpublished memorandum.

The effort to refine the scope and quality concept is significant, but the resulting redefinition of workload produced some peculiar results, particularly for welfare. Since the proportion of the population below the poverty line declined in the period 1954-69, the use of this definition yields a decline in workload of 39.4 percent, when, in fact, the numbers and proportions of families on welfare were increasing rapidly.

Reischauer's estimates also showed an insignificant increase in the scope and quality of highways for the 1955-69 period. This was a period of very great expansion in the highway network in this country, and an estimated decline in scope and quality would appear to be a peculiar, if not misleading, finding. Again, this appears to be a workload measurement problem.

The next effort in this area appeared as an appendix to an address given by Dr. Andrew F. Brimmer, member of the Board of Governors of the Federal Reserve System, at Middlebury College on May 30, 1971.[9] Two statistical series are presented for the years 1955-69 and for 1965-69. The components are "workload," "price," and "scope and quality," utilizing the Reischauer concepts of these terms.

The most recent effort in this area was done by the Council of Economic Advisers of the state of New York. Except for some minor differences in their cost indexes, they employed Reischauer's method. Table 5-2 reproduces their results.

For both the 1957-70 and the 1965-70 time periods, in all cases changes in workload were less important in New York than in the nation as a whole. As a result, the scope and quality residual was more important. Where possible, separate estimates were provided for scope and for quality. In both time periods, increases in quality accounted for more than 20 percent of the increase in expenditures for those three functions where scope and quality could be separated. From these estimates, the Council concluded that

state and local governments in New York, much more than in the nation at large, have met the rise in workload and the often steep climb in the cost of public services, and have gone beyond that to provide service to more of the population.[10]

The foregoing brief review of previous research efforts in this area—the estimation of the components of change in state-local government expenditures—indicates that there are severe problems in this type of analysis. One of these is the assumption that over the period examined there are constant returns to scale. The empirical research that has been done does not lead to strong conclusions on economies and diseconomies of scale in local government functions.[11] Thus it appears that the assumption of constant returns must be used until additional research suggests alternative assumptions.

A second troublesome assumption is that of constant factor proportions over time in local government service provision. Here, as noted in Chapter 3, the pervasive difficulty is the absence of reliable measures of local government capital flows.

A third difficulty, well-reflected in the previous research in this area, is in the definition of workload. Population served is not a very satisfactory concept when that population is nonhomogeneous over time. And since local governments operate in a spatial context where the provision of services is not uniform over the area some of the population will be "better served" than others.

A fourth difficulty is the cost index. Ideally, a specific index should be constructed for each specific service in each jurisdiction. This is an impossible task, and the analyst is thus forced to employ some proxy measurements of cost. Fortunately, it is possible to find some reasonably good proxies so that operationally this problem is not intractable.

Finally the residual—traditionally designated as scope and quality—is most difficult to interpret. It contains an error term, reflecting any imperfections in cost and workload measurement, and it combines productivity changes and quality changes.

Table 5-2

Percentage of Increase in Expenditures Attributable to Increase in Workload, Price, Scope and Quality–New York and U.S. State and Local Governments, 1957-70

			1957-70						1965-70		
	Work-load	Price	Scope	Quality	Scope & Quality	Work-load	Price	Scope	Quality	Scope & Quality
	(1)	(2)	(3)	(4)	(5)	(6)	(7)	(8)	(9)	(10)
United States										
Total General Expenditure	24.4	42.8	–	–	32.8	14.5	49.2	–	–	36.2
Local Schools	24.3	48.7	6.8	20.2	27.0	10.2	54.6	6.6	28.6	35.2
Administration & Other	16.1	39.7	–	–	44.2	9.5	46.5	–	–	44.0
Public Welfare	a	23.8	58.6	17.6	76.2	a	23.0	70.4	6.6	77.0
Urban Services	27.5	50.7	–	–	21.8	27.8	61.3	–	–	10.8
Hospitals and Health	17.3	44.9	–	–	37.8	9.0	47.0	–	–	43.9
Higher & Misc. Education	31.8	32.7	30.2	5.3	35.5	26.1	33.4	40.0	.5	40.5
Highways	52.1	47.9	b	b	b	39.8	60.2	b	b	b
New York State										
Total General Expenditure	16.3	42.0	–	–	41.7	7.1	44.6	–	–	48.3
Local Schools	23.1	44.3	8.8	23.8	32.6	9.4	52.4	9.6	28.6	38.2
Administration & Other	10.7	38.9	–	–	50.4	4.6	38.5	–	–	56.9
Public Welfare	a	20.6	55.6	23.9	79.5	a	17.6	54.5	28.0	82.5
Urban Services	13.3	63.2	–	–	23.5	6.1	79.8	–	–	14.1
Hospitals and Health	11.3	43.6	–	–	45.1	4.8	40.8	–	–	54.5
Higher & Misc. Education	23.9	26.0	25.8	24.3	50.1	24.6	34.3	14.2	26.9	41.1
Highways	46.7	53.3	b	b	b	36.3	63.7	b	b	b

aDecline in workload, instead of an increase, treated as zero contribution to increased expenditure.

bScope and/or quality declined with a resultant decline in the two combined, with the contribution to increased expenditure from scope and/or quality treated as zero.

Note: In expenditures where scope and quality can be determined individually, the combined scope and quality of column (5) and of (10) equals the sum of (3) and (4), and of (8) and (9) respectively.

Computations by New York State Council of Economic Advisers, based on data from various sources including New York State Departments of Commerce, Education, Health; Social Services; and the Division of the Budget; and United States Departments of Commerce; Health, Education, and Welfare; Transportation; and the Office of Economic Opportunity.

Source: Council of Economic Advisers, State of New York, *Annual Report* (Albany 1972), p. 19.

And, to complicate matters further, there may be some significant behavioral interactions among cost, workload, quality, and productivity. These may include both the behavior of administrators who are operating under severe budget constraints, the behavior of hard-pressed taxpayers, and the behavior of the beneficiaries of local government services. These kinds of considerations will be examined below.

Nevertheless, and in spite of all the conceptual and measurement difficulties in this approach to the analysis of local government expenditures, efforts to refine the technique may produce useful results. In a given pattern of revenue constraints, government expenditures *are* determined by cost, workload, and by the quality of the service provided. Moreover, budget officers approach their tasks in this context. Budget-making typically starts with measures of past and current year cost and workload, and estimates of cost and workload for the budget year. The budgetmaker then adds on the new services that must be provided or makes allowances for an improved quality of inputs. Thus this approach to the analysis of changes in local government expenditures, unlike the determinants studies, is in an operational context.

Some of the difficulties associated with returns to scale, factor proportions, and workload measurements would be less formidable if local governments compiled data on their operations on a consistent annual basis over a period of time. This would permit analysis over two- or three-year periods and contribute to budget-making on a continuous basis.

Measuring the Contribution of Cost, Workload, and the Residual

The approach used in this study is in many ways similar to the one used in previous efforts to analyze changes in government expenditures over a given period of time. The initial (1959) and terminal (1969) years will be denoted $t = 1$ and $t = 2$ respectively. Expenditures, E_t, will be expressed as functions of costs, C_t, and workload, W_t.[12]

C_t will be used to represent the public-sector analogue of the cost of inputs and W_t the public-sector analogue of the outputs of government activity. Costs will be stated in terms of an index and the cost index will be derived, as far as possible, from the cost of a basic, relatively homogeneous input that has a high positive linear correlation with cost trends. In elementary and secondary education, for example, this could be the salary of the entering teacher with a fresh B.A.; in welfare, the entering salary of the newly hired caseworker combined with price-adjusted welfare payments; in police and fire, the entering salary.[13] Current costs of materials and annual capital costs will be deflated where appropriate for specific functions.

In general, workload (W_t) will be defined as "population served." The number of students in elementary and secondary public schools is such a measure; the number of persons on the rolls define workload for welfare. Alternative definitions of workload are examined in Chapter 6.

The basic algebraic relation employed in the work of Robinson and Reischauer is:

$$\frac{E_2}{E_1} = \left(\frac{C_2}{C_1}\right) \left(\frac{W_2}{W_1}\right) \left(\frac{R_2}{R_1}\right)$$

This can be rewritten as follows:

$$\frac{R_2}{R_1} = \frac{E_2}{E_1 \left(\frac{C_2}{C_1}\right) \left(\frac{W_2}{W_1}\right)}$$

The term

$$E_1 \left(\frac{C_2}{C_1}\right) \left(\frac{W_2}{W_1}\right)$$

represents an *estimate* of expenditure for the terminal year based solely on actual expenditure in the initial year and changes in the cost and workload factors over the period. Hence, an anticipated or *projected value* for expenditure in the terminal year will be defined.

Definition 5-1: $P(E_2) = E_1 \left(\frac{C_2}{C_1}\right) \left(\frac{W_2}{W_1}\right)$

The *difference* between *actual* expenditure in the terminal year and the estimate of expenditure will be denoted by R^*.

Definition 5-2: $R^* = E_2 - P(E_2)$

Thus the *residual* R^* is the portion of the actual expenditure, E_2, that is occasioned by factors other than changes in cost and workload; these include changes in productivity, changes in quality, and an error component. The residual R^* is the portion of actual expenditures (E_2) that is not explained by changes in cost and workload. The residual must be further examined by means of proxy measures of quality and productivity (see below).

The relation between the residual R^*, as defined here, and the "scope and quality" factor R_2/R_1 as used by Reischauer is obtained as follows:

$$\frac{R_2}{R_1} = \frac{E_2}{E_1 \left(\frac{C_2}{C_1}\right)\left(\frac{W_2}{W_1}\right)} = \frac{E_2}{P(E_2)} \qquad \text{[Def. 5-1]}$$

$$\frac{R_2}{R_1} - 1 = \frac{E_2}{P(E_2)} - 1 = \frac{E_2 - P(E_2)}{P(E_2)} = \frac{R^*}{P(E_2)} \qquad \text{[Def. 5-2]}$$

$$R^* = P(E_2)\left(\frac{R_2}{R_1} - 1\right)$$

Since actual expenditure, E_2, may be less than, equal to, or greater than the projected value $P(E_2)$, the corresponding values for R^* and R_2/R_1 are:

$$E_2 < P(E_2) \qquad R^* < 0 \qquad \frac{R_2}{R_1} < 1$$

$$E_2 = P(E_2) \qquad R^* = 0 \qquad \frac{R_2}{R_1} = 1$$

$$E_2 > P(E_2) \qquad R^* > 0 \qquad \frac{R_2}{R_1} > 1$$

When $E_2 < P(E_2)$ the nonerror component of R^* may mean a decrease in quality, an increase in productivity, or some combination of the two. When $E_2 > P(E_2)$ the nonerror component of R^* may mean an increase in quality, a decrease in productivity, or, again, some combination of the two. The problem of interpreting the residual R^* will be discussed below.

Partitioning the Components of
Changes in Expenditure

The next step is to assign weights to the components of the change in expenditure: cost, workload, and the residual. The actual change in expenditure is $\Delta E = E_2 - E_1$.

Definition 5-3: $\Delta c = \dfrac{C_2}{C_1} - 1$ and $\Delta w = \dfrac{W_2}{W_1} - 1$

Hence $\dfrac{C_2}{C_1} = (1 + \Delta c)$ and $\dfrac{W_2}{W_1} = (1 + \Delta w)$

The development of the partitioning equation is summarized in the following sequence of equations. In the partition of the "cross-product term," $E_1 (\Delta c \Delta w)$, absolute values of the quantities Δc and Δw are used to obtain a proportional weighting of the effect of the changes in cost and workload.

$$E_2 = R^* + P(E_2)$$ [Def. 5-2]

$$E_2 - E_1 = R^* + P(E_2) - E_1$$

$$P(E_2) = E_1(1 + \Delta c)(1 + \Delta w) = E_1 + E_2(\Delta c + \Delta w + \Delta c \Delta w)$$

[Def. 5-1, 5-2, and 5-3]

$$\Delta E = R^* + E_1(\Delta c + \Delta w + \Delta c \Delta w) = R^* + E_1 \Delta c + E_1 \Delta w + E_1(\Delta c \Delta w)$$

$$E_1(\Delta c \Delta w) = E_1(\Delta c \Delta w) \; [\frac{|\Delta c|}{|\Delta c| + |\Delta w|} + \frac{|\Delta w|}{|\Delta c| \quad |\Delta w|}]$$

(partitioning the "cross-product term")

$$\Delta E = R^* + E_1 \; [\Delta c + \Delta c \Delta w (\frac{|\Delta c|}{|\Delta c| + |\Delta w|})]$$

$$+ E_1 \; [\Delta w + \Delta c \Delta w (\frac{|\Delta w|}{|\Delta c| + |\Delta w|})]$$

Thus the change in expenditure is the sum of a residual component and projected cost and workload components. Finally, the percentage distribution for the residual, cost, and workload components is obtained by dividing the partitioning equation by the absolute value of ΔE and multiplying by 100.

A few hypothetical cases illustrate the use of the procedure (see Table 5-3). The details of the calculations for the first case in Table 5-3 are:

$$P(E_2) = (1000)(1.5)(0.9) = 1350$$

$$R^* = 1400 - 1350 = 50$$

$$\Delta E = 1400 - 1000 = 400$$

$$\Delta c = (1.5 - 1) = 0.5 \text{ and } \Delta w = (0.9 - 1) = -0.1$$

$$\frac{|0.5|}{|0.5| + |-0.1|} = \frac{0.5}{0.6} = \frac{5}{6} \quad \text{and} \quad \frac{|-0.1|}{|0.5| + |-0.1|} = \frac{0.1}{0.6} = \frac{1}{6}$$

$$400 = 50 + 1000[0.5) + (0.5)(-0.1)(5/6)] + 1000[(-0.1 + (0.5)(-0.1)(1/6)]$$

$$400 = 50 + (500 - 41.7) + (-100 - 8.3)$$

$$400 = 50 + 458.3 - 108.3$$

$$1 = 0.125 + 1.145 - 0.27 \quad \text{(divide above equation by 400)}$$

Table 5-3
Selected Cases to Illustrate Partitioning Procedure

	E_1	C_2/C_1	W_2/W_1	$P(E_2)$	E_2	R^*
Case 1	1000	1.5	0.9	1350	1400	50
Case 2	1000	1.5	1.1	1650	1700	50
Case 3	1000	0.75	0.67	500	450	−50

	Change in Expenditure	Percent Attributable to Components		
	ΔE	R^*	C	W
Case 1	400	12.5	114.5	−27.0
Case 2	700	7.1	77.4	15.7
Case 3	−550	−9.0	−39.0	−52.0

Interpreting the Residual

One component in the residual is an improvement in quality, which has been the conventional interpretation. This means that additional expenditures (beyond projected expenditures) are for higher quality inputs, or better services, or a wider range of services. But unfortunately, in all cases where E_2 exceeds $P(E_2)$, there may not be a resulting increase in the quality of the public program. Payrolls may have been padded with incompetent employees; additional expenditures may not always be equated with an improvement in quality.

Equating increased government expenditure with increased quality of government services may not always conform with a citizen-taxpayer view of government activities, but it does, typically, conform with a government official's view of government activities. There are very few bureau or division administrators in any government who do not feel that more inputs yield a higher quality output of government services.

Another component of the residual is a change in productivity, defined as above in terms of a change in output per man-year, or, in cost terms, as a cost reduction per unit of workload. If expenditure, after adjustment for cost and workload, continues to increase, this may mean that productivity declines. Therefore positive values of R^* may be interpreted as either an *increase* in quality or a *decline* in productivity or some mixture of the two. Similarly, negative values of R^* may be interpreted as either a *decline* in quality, or an *increase* in productivity, or some mixture of the two.

It is also possible that productivity increases are reflected in changes in the cost index as well as in the residual. For example, if labor is becoming more productive, that is, output per man-year is increasing and labor-capital ratios are unchanged, the marginal productivity of labor is rising. If public-sector wage rates are roughly related to the marginal productivity of labor inputs, wage rates will rise, and this will be reflected in the cost index as an increase in starting salaries. But if labor productivity increases, this also means that fewer employees are necessary to handle the same workload, with a corresponding reduction in expenditure. In such cases it is necessary to examine cost, workload, and the number of employees to determine if there has been a productivity increase.

Grant-in-Aid Impacts

There is no way by which the influence of state and federal aid on local expenditures can be estimated in this examination of the components of expenditure change. Federal and state aid can add to local expenditures, can lead to substitution effects (aid for education can be deflected to health, for example), or can lead to local tax reduction. Moreover, impacts will differ by type of jurisdiction, as between central cities and outside central city areas, and among programs. Again, the considerable amount of research that has been done on this problem leads to divergent and complex conclusions.[14]

The analysis of federal and state aid impacts is particularly significant if projections are undertaken for future patterns of local expenditure, which is not the case here. For present purposes, although it would be helpful if such impacts could be traced directly, it need only be assumed that the aid impacts have been reflected in local expenditure decisions and hence "incorporated" in the historical record of expenditure patterns. No attempt will be made to estimate the "component" effect of aid in a manner comparable to the way in which workload, cost, and quality will be estimated.

Behavioral Interactions

In an operational sense, workload, cost and the residual may not be truly independent, one of the other, in the manner that must be assumed. For example, when taxpayers revolt and school budgets are cut or held to minimal increases, school administrators may respond in different ways. Expenditure increases may be minimized by reducing entering teachers' salaries, which will be reflected in the cost index. Expenditures may be minimized by cutting back auxiliary personnel, which will be reflected in the residual. Expenditures may be minimized by cutting workload, such as refusing to admit transfer students from other school districts.

The operational interaction among cost, workload, and the residual is probably even higher with respect to welfare. Here the administrator, faced with a tight budget constraint, may discharge caseworkers, thus reducing the quality of case work, may refuse to raise entering salaries of caseworkers, affecting the cost index, may tighten the restrictions on welfare qualifications, thus reducing the workload, or may eliminate some of the welfare "extras" such as a clothing allowance for children at the beginning of the school term, again reducing the quality (level) of welfare benefits. Thus the model must necessarily assume that cost, workload, and the residual are independent, but in the operational world of local government they are most certainly not independent. Again, the numbers reflect decisions that are a part of history. Projections would be hazardous.

There are other operational interactions that are neglected in this approach to the measurement of changes in local government expenditure. The availability of revenue constrains local government expenditure, much more than for the states or the national government. Also, this approach does not examine directly the presence or absence of a local government infrastructure, and how it has been financed. The decisions of previous generations to borrow for capital outlay will commit the current generation to the payment of interest and amortization. This will further limit current account expenditure.

It would be very useful to translate an analysis of changes in local government expenditures into statewide per capita terms and aggregate across functions. If governmental expenditures per capita have increased it would seem reasonable that the "average" citizen is entitled to know the causes of such increase. Unfortunately, such an average per capita figure is almost meaningless. The differences among local governments in the delivery of services—police, fire, sanitation, health, education, welfare, and so forth—with respect to quantity and quality in their spatial dimensions and jurisdictional dimensions, are so sharp as to make a per capita figure misleading.

Final Steps: Proxy Measures

Since the residual embraces both productivity and quality change, it is necessary to undertake an independent examination of whatever measures are available in an attempt to interpret the residual. One approach to this problem is to identify that part of the change in the residual which is attributable to changes in quality and partition it out. The principal difficulty this approach must face is that without a direct price, there is no necessary agreement as to what constitutes an improvement in quality. The most prevalent procedure for determining quality changes is to identify quantifiable proxies. But who is to identify these proxies? Three different groups may be involved: the analyst, the government administrator, or the general public. Since the choice of proxies is basically a matter of value judgment, there is no reason for these three groups to agree.

Even assuming that there is general agreement on certain quality proxies, how are the different proxies to be weighted? Should all proxies that can be identified receive equal weight or should some be given a greater weight in determining quality change? Without an output price, there is no objective method for weighting the different quality proxies.

In spite of these difficulties, three methods can be suggested for disaggregating the residual. The first is to simply assume that quality has remained constant. Then the entire residual is attributed to changes in productivity. This is the assumption used in studies of federal government productivity. The second method is to identify a set of quality proxies for each service and note the direction and magnitude of the changes in these proxies. This method will not empirically disaggregate the residual, but it will provide a great deal of insight into the direction and probable magnitude of the productivity component of the residual.

The third method was implied by Bradford, Malt, and Oates in their study.[15] It is a crude deflation method. Quality proxies are identified. Then any change in the identified proxy is used to deflate the residual. After deflation has taken place, the remaining residual is attributed to productivity. This method is rather rough; it weights all quality changes equally.

Thus a completely satisfactory method for disaggregating the residual does not yet exist. At this stage, using all three methods yields the best examination of the components of the residual. These techniques will be utilized in the following chapter.

6

Cost, Workload, Quality, and Productivity

The technique elaborated in the preceding chapter will be employed here to analyze selected changes in local government expenditure in New York State between the years 1959 and 1969.

The first step is to estimate the amount of change to be attributed to workload and the amount to be attributed to cost, leaving an unexplained residual that may be either positive or negative. This residual reflects changes in quality, changes in productivity, or a combination of the two. Thus the final step is to analyze the residual.

The approach used here explicitly introduces a concept of "projected value." Assume that in 1959 the expenditure for a specific government unit was $100 and that by 1969 the workload of the unit had doubled and the cost of its inputs had also doubled. Then, on the basis of workload and cost alone, it may be projected that expenditure in 1969 would be $400. But suppose that actual expenditure in 1969 is $450. The difference between expected and actual is the residual to be explained. It may be explained by an *improvement* in the quality of the government service provided. It may also be explained by a *decrease* in the productivity of the government unit.

The concept of projected value is contained in the following:

$$\frac{\text{Expenditure in 1969}}{\text{Expenditure in 1959}} = \frac{\text{Workload in 1969}}{\text{Workload in 1959}} \times \frac{\text{Cost in 1969}}{\text{Cost in 1959}} \times \frac{\text{Quality \& Productivity in 1969}}{\text{Quality \& Productivity in 1959}}.$$

The local government functions that are examined here are, for the state as a whole, education and welfare—the largest components of local government expenditure. For these statewide functions, New York City will be treated separately from other local governments.

Police protection and fire protection are examined for New York City and the five largest upstate cities. It is not possible in New York State to analyze the police function outside of major cities because of the overlapping jurisdictions of town and village police, county police, and the New York State police. Fire protection is likewise susceptible to analysis only for cities; volunteer fire departments in towns and some villages cannot be examined on a cost and workload basis.

Some economists have estimated cost, workload, and quality-productivity changes for an aggregate of functions described as "general urban services" or have used an "all other" category. The position taken here is that such aggregations are much too broad to be meaningful.

109

Workload is measured in terms of population served—for education the number of children in school, for welfare the number on welfare rolls, for police the population within the jurisdiction examined, for fire protection the full value of property.

Cost is measured in terms of homogeneous inputs. For education, personnel costs are measured in terms of the starting salary of the beginning teacher with a B.A. degree. Police personnel costs are measured by the starting salary of the patrolman. Welfare costs are divided into two major components: administrative costs and welfare payments. The salary of the entering caseworker is used for the first component. Other details on sources of data are described in Appendixes A and B. The second part of this chapter examines selected aspects of government service provision in Onondaga County—Syracuse.

New York Local Government Experience

Table 6-1 shows the percentage increase in current expenditure between 1959 and 1969 for elementary and secondary education, welfare, police, and fire. For education and welfare, the state, New York City, and the state exclusive of New York City are independently examined. The increase in current expenditure for the police and fire functions are reported for the six largest cities in New York—New York City, Buffalo, Rochester, Albany, Syracuse, and Yonkers. New York City and the other five cities are then analyzed separately. The final three columns of Table 6-1 estimate the percentage of these expenditure increases which may be attributed to the increase in workload, cost, and quality-productivity.

For example, current expenditure for education in New York State increased by 206.5 percent from 1959 to 1969. Changes in workload, in this case number of pupils enrolled, accounted for 20.5 percent of this increase. If all other factors had remained constant, and only the number of pupils enrolled had increased, expenditures on education would have increased by about 41 percent (20 percent of 206). The increase in cost—the average basic salary of the starting teacher—contributed 36.8 percent of the expenditure increase. Finally, 42.7 percent of the expenditure increase is left as an unexplained residual—unexplained in that neither measured changes in workload nor cost contributed to this part of the change in expenditure. This residual reflects a significant change in the educational service provided in the state. Either the quality of education increased over the decade or the productivity of providing the service within the state declined, making it more costly to provide each unit of education.

Thus an increase in the quality-productivity residual shows either an increase in quality, a decrease in productivity, or some combination of the two. If this category is positive, it means that the actual expenditure is greater than would be expected given the changes in workload and cost. Some characteristics of the service, other than workload or cost, have changed.

Table 6-1
The Sources of the Increase in Local Expenditure, 1959-69[a]

	Increase in Current Expenditure (in Thousands)	Percentage Increase in Current Expenditure	Percentage of Increase in Expenditure Attributable to the Increase in		
			Workload	Cost	Quality Productivity
Education					
New York State	$2,630,196	206.5	20.5	36.8	42.7
New York City	844,396	189.6	9.1	31.5	59.4
State without New York City	1,785,800	215.7	21.7	37.3	40.9
Welfare					
New York State	2,028,473	528.8	62.1	9.6	28.3
New York City	1,493,749	594.6	60.5	8.6	30.9
State without New York City	534,724	403.8	68.1	12.7	19.2
Police					
Six Major Cities	308,869	182.5	0.0	89.4	10.6
New York City	295,398	193.6	0.8	89.4	9.8
Five Upstate Cities	13,470	81.1	−10.6	62.5	48.1
Fire					
Six Major Cities	144,280	159.4	99.2	156.1	−155.3
New York City	125,605	163.5	113.8	174.5	−188.3
Five Upstate Cities	18,675	136.2	30.0	51.8	18.1

[a]See Appendix A for data sources.

Of the four functions examined, elementary and secondary education shows the highest positive increase in the quality-productivity residual. For the state as a whole, changes in the component account for 42.7 percent of the total change in current education expenditure. This is a much larger quality-productivity increase for New York State than for the nation as a whole. (See Table 5-1.) A part of this difference may be attributable to the definition of workload and cost, and the difference in the time period covered by these two studies. There is also the possibility that the quality of education provided in New York State increased relatively more than for the nation, or that productivity in the provision of education declined relatively more in New York State.

For New York City changes in quality-productivity in education account for 59.4 percent of the change in expenditure as compared to 40.9 percent attributable to this category for the state without New York City. Although New York City had a slightly smaller percentage increase in current expenditure, their percentage increase in workload was less than half of that for the rest of the state. The result is that a larger percentage of the expenditure increase in New York City education is attributed to changes in the quality-productivity residual than for the rest of the state.

Increases in workload explain the majority of the increase in current expenditure for welfare. For the state as a whole, workload accounts for 62.1 percent of the increase in expenditure, while quality-productivity accounts for only 28.3 percent of this increase. The difference between these results and those in Table 5-1 for the nation is primarily a consequence of the change in the definition of workload. Here *workload* is defined as the number of persons receiving welfare, without reference to the proportions of families below the poverty line. Quality-productivity explains only 28.3 percent of the increase in expenditure for New York State as compared to 70.3 percent for the nation as a whole.

The concept of a workload for the police force is particularly difficult to quantify. The police function is primarily a preventive service, but it is impossible to measure the number of crimes, accidents, or imprudent activities prevented by the police. Crime statistics, which may be viewed as a sort of negative preventive measure, are not a good workload measure. Both reporting systems and decisions as to when to arrest or not arrest vary over time among communities and within communities.

In certain instances there are other statistics that may possibly be used to measure workload. An example is the number of "radio runs" in New York City. This figure increased by more than 100 percent over the period. If this is a proper measure for workload, the percentage increase in current expenditure attributable to quality-productivity becomes negative, indicating an increase in productivity. Unfortunately, data on the number of radio runs are not available for the other five cities. Therefore, to be consistent, the workload for police is defined as the population of the city.

This measure probably understates the actual workload of the police department. One certainly does not have to be a resident of the city to commit a crime in the city, or in the more obvious case, add to traffic congestion. The socioeconomic mix of the population is also important in determining the workload of police. Even if the actual number of city residents remains the same, if the mix changes, the workload may either rise or fall.

The cost index is based on the starting salary, including all fringe benefits except retirement, for the starting patrolman.[a] In the six major cities, in New York City, and in the five upstate cities cost increases account for the majority of the increase in expenditure. Only New York City had a slight increase in expenditure attributable to a change in workload. The changes in quality-productivity contributed a sizable portion of the change in expenditure only in the five upstate cities where population actually declined.

---

[a]Retirement is omitted because it was not possible to secure reliable estimates for the 1959-69 period.

Fire is the last function analyzed. Since fire protection is also a preventive service, workload is again very difficult to measure. For this study, *workload* is defined in terms of equalized property values for each city, on the assumption that the primary responsibility of a fire department is to protect property. The cost index is based on the change in starting salaries of firemen. All fringe benefits except retirement are included.[b] New York City had large increases in both workload and cost. As a result, the increase in current expenditure attributable to quality-productivity declined. The five upstate cities show relatively moderate increases in both workload and cost; thus 18.1 percent of the increase in their expenditure is attributable to quality-productivity. In all cases, increases in cost made up the major component of the increase in current expenditure.

The difference between the change in police expenditure attributable to cost increase and the change in fire expenditure attributable to cost increase in New York City is a result of the method used to divide the expenditure increases. This method requires that the components—workload, cost, and quality-productivity—account for 100 percent of the expenditure change. *Workload* for police is defined as population served, whereas for fire it is defined as equalized property value. The *cost* for both police and fire is defined as the entering salary of the patrolman or fireman. The difference in the amount of the expenditure increase attributable to cost in these two functions is a result of the sharply differing definition of workload.

The choice of equalized property values as an appropriate measure of workload for fire protection illustrates some of the significant aspects of the methodology employed in this approach to productivity measurement. In terms of the results that emerge, it is evident that property values have increased much more rapidly in New York City than in the five upstate cities. It is also possible that the New York City findings—which suggest a major improvement in productivity over the period—are somewhat suspect because of changes in property-tax equalization procedures. However, if the assumption is accepted that the protection of property values is the major mission of a fire department, then fire protection in New York City has indeed experienced a major improvement in productivity over the period.

Separating Quality and Productivity

Although there are no completely satisfactory ways to separate the quality-productivity component of these expenditure increases, three procedures were suggested in Chapter 5. First, the example of the federal government productivity studies may be followed. Here the assumption is that no change in quality has occurred. This procedure would allocate the entire change in expenditure

---

[b]Again, the reason for neglecting retirement is the lack of reliable data.

attributable to quality-productivity to a change in productivity. The second method is to identify quality proxies for each service, examine the direction in which these proxies have changed, and, using that information, draw inferences regarding the direction of productivity change. Of the three methods, this second method, although not exact, does yield the best insights into the quality-productivity dimension.

The third procedure is a crude "deflating" method. In this approach any numerical quality change that can be identified is used to deflate the quality-productivity residual. After deflating for these quality changes, the remainder of the residual is attributed to changes in productivity. In an attempt to separate the quality-productivity residual, each of these three procedures will be undertaken.

Method I. This method assumes that the quality of each service remains constant over the ten years studied. Thus any change in expenditure not accounted for by changes in either workload or cost is the result of a change in productivity. For example, from 1959 to 1969 current expenditure for elementary and secondary education in New York State increased by 206.5 percent. If quality had remained constant, and only the productivity of the provision of education changed, productivity would have fallen by 42.7 percent over the ten-year period (see Table 6-1).

Using this method, the only gain in productivity was in New York City fire prevention. That service had a major gain of 188.3 percent in productivity over the ten-year period.

These estimates of productivity losses, except for fire, appear to be much too large to be considered reliable. Intuitively, one would expect that the quality of the services improved to some extent. Thus method I for separating quality-productivity should be rejected as a definitive technique for separating quality and productivity.

Method II. With method II quality proxies are identified for each service. This method does not attempt to separate quantitatively changes in quality from changes in productivity, but it does identify changes in some quality proxies. In doing so, it provides insight into the probable change in productivity.

One of the major difficulties encountered in estimating changes in quality is the paucity of data that can be used as quality proxies. In consequence, only a limited number of quality proxies can be identified for each function. Two quality proxies were identified for education for the entire state and three were identified for welfare. For police one quality proxy was identified for both New York City and the five upstate cities. One quality proxy was identified for fire in New York City while two proxies were identified for the five upstate cities.

For the quality of education, the first proxy used is the ratio of instructional personnel to pupils. An increase in this ratio should indicate an increase in the quality of education. The results show a rise in ratio of instructional personnel per pupil of 18.1 percent, indicating some increase in the quality of education for the state.

The holding power of the public high school is the second quality proxy for education. This proxy measures the percentage of high school students who graduate within three years after completing the ninth grade. If this percentage increases, the quality of education may be said to have improved. In 1958-59, 66.6 percent of New York State students graduated within three years, while in 1968-69, 73.5 percent graduated within three years. This proxy indicates an improvement in the quality of education within the state.

Both of these quality proxies indicate substantial increases in the quality of education in the state. These calculations suggest that at least some, but probably not all, of the changes in current expenditure for education that have been attributable to changes in quality-productivity may be accounted for by changes in the quality of education.

Three proxies are used to indicate changes in the quality of welfare. The first is the change in the ratio of welfare employees per welfare recipient. Assuming that more caseworkers and staff improve the welfare services provided, an increase in this ratio implies an increase in the quality of the service. The results show a decline in this ratio of 28.1 percent, which is interpreted here as a decline in the quality of welfare service for the state as a whole.

A second proxy is the ratio of welfare recipients to the number of families and unrelated individuals below the poverty line. An increase in this ratio suggests that the quality of welfare service has improved in that more needy persons are now covered. The increase here of 219.0 percent indicates a substantial quality increase in welfare. Thus welfare quality, if defined in this way, has certainly improved.

The most significant measure of the quality of welfare service must surely rest on either the proportion of the poor who are covered by welfare—which has increased in New York State—or the real income of welfare beneficiaries. This last measure indicates that the average welfare recipient has had a very small improvement in his real welfare payment over the decade 1959-69. For the state as a whole, the average welfare recipient had an annual improvement in his real income position (from welfare) of less than 1 percent a year. The real income improvement of the average welfare recipient outside New York City was slightly better than that of the average welfare recipient in New York City.

It may be noted that the concept of "average welfare recipient" is difficult to define. In the estimates here some categories of assistance, such as foster care, are eliminated and persons rather than families are utilized for averaging purposes.

Thus welfare coverage increased and real welfare payments per recipient remained almost constant over the decade. The coverage dimension is highly positive; the quality dimension in terms of the real income of recipients remains virtually constant. Restating the relationship another way—the average welfare recipient is very little better off than in 1959, but coverage has increased. The average recipient is not improving his real income by means of welfare, but more families and single individuals have been covered. If one looks at coverage, quality has increased, and, in all likelihood, productivity has remained the same. If one looks at per person real income, quality is virtually unchanged and productivity is reduced.

The sole proxy used for police is the ratio of policemen to population. A rising ratio indicates more police per person and, presumably, an increase in the quality of the police service. For New York City, this ratio increased by 18.5 percent. The five upstate cities experienced a decline in this ratio of 1.7 percent, indicating a slight fall in the quality of the police service. These results suggest some increase in the quality of the police function for New York City, and the possibility of a decline in the productivity of police in the five upstate cities. In these cities, over 48 percent of the increase in expenditure is attributable to changes in quality-productivity. Thus a decline in the productivity of the police service in the five cities seems the most reasonable conclusion.

In certain instances, other quality proxies are available. For example, the installation of the emergency call number, 911, in New York City makes police more available and in that sense improves the quality of the service. This number received more than 6 million calls in 1969, but the extent of the quality increase due to the emergency call number is impossible to measure. This system was not used in 1959 and therefore there is no comparable data for that year. Also, it is not possible to sort out the number of 911 calls that actually pertain to the police function.

The proxy used to indicate the quality of fire services is the ratio of firemen to equalized property values. An increase in this ratio should indicate an increase in quality. For New York City this ratio fell by 40.9 percent, again indicating a decline in quality. The negative sign of the fire residual indicates either a *decline* in quality or an *increase* in productivity. In this case the quality decline accounts for some but probably not all of the expenditure attributable to the residual. Thus productivity undoubtedly increased for this function.

For the five upstate cities, the ratio of firemen to equalized property values fell by 11.5 percent, again indicating a decline in quality. Given the positive sign of the quality-productivity residual, these results indicate a decline in the productivity of fire service provided in the upstate cities.[c]

An independent measure of the quality of fire protection in New York cities is provided by the "key rate" established by the New York Fire Insurance Rating Organization. The "key rate" is based on an evaluation by the Rating Organization of such factors as the adequacy of water supply and the adequacy of fire-fighting equipment. It is expressed in terms of cents per thousand dollars

[c]Once again, these findings rest heavily on the acceptance of equalized property values as an appropriate measure of workload.

of insured value. It is available for the five upstate cities, but there is no "key rate" for New York City.

For the five upstate cities, the key rate changed very slightly between 1959 and 1969. For Syracuse and Yonkers, the key rate increased from $0.19 to $0.20 per $1,000 of insured value. In Albany, the rate increased from $0.25 to $0.26, and in Buffalo from $0.18 to $0.20. Only in Rochester did the rate remain constant at $0.18 over the period. The changes in these key rates again indicate a slight deterioration in the quality of fire service provided for all of these cities except Rochester. This finding reinforces the possibility that productivity in the fire function fell in these five cities over the period studied.

Method III. The third suggested method for separating quality-productivity involves a crude type of deflation for changes in quality. After such a deflation, the remaining residual is attributed to changes in productivity. For example, assume that the teacher/pupil ratio increased by 10 percent and the quality-productivity residual had increased by 20 percent. If the residual is deflated for the quality increase by dividing 1.20 by 1.10 then the remaining 9.1 percent residual change is attributed to a decline in productivity.

The ratio of persons employed to population served is the only quality proxy which is consistently used for all four services, and is therefore the only proxy used for deflation. Table 6-2 reports the results.

Like method I, this approach does not seem to adequately account for changes in quality. Thus the estimated productivity changes must be rejected; the deflation procedure is simply too crude.

Table 6-2
Method III: Deflated for Quality Change,[a] 1959-69

	Percentage Change in Expenditure Resulting from a Change in Productivity (Assuming No Quality Change)	Percentage Change in Quality	Percentage Change in Expenditure Resulting from a Change in Productivity Deflated for Quality Changes
Education			
New York State	59.4	18.1	74.6
Welfare			
New York State	247.5	−28.1	208.3
Police			
New York City	0.4	18.5	16.0
Five Upstate Cities	41.4	−1.7	39.7
Fire			
New York City	−251.2	−40.8	−182.2
Five Upstate Cities	40.8	−11.5	27.7

[a]A positive change in expenditure implies a decline in productivity.

Review of Results

The above analysis demonstrates the difficulties involved in separating quality and productivity changes. Of the three methods, method II seems to provide the most insight into changes in productivity. It indicates that there have been some quality improvements in both education and police, although probably not enough to account for the large change in expenditure attributable to quality-productivity. This analysis indicates that productivity has probably fallen slightly, or at best remained constant, for these two services over this period. The quality of welfare has improved very little, if at all, over this period. Given the size of the residual, productivity may have even fallen slightly for this function. For New York City, the quality proxy employed for fire declined. Given the negative residual, productivity has improved for New York City fire provision. For the five upstate cities, quality fell and the residual was positive, indicating a decline in·productivity in the provision of the fire service in these five cities.

Onondaga County-Syracuse Experience

The cost, workload, quality-productivity technique was also applied to selected governmental services in Onondaga County and the City of Syracuse to ascertain if additional insights can be gained at a lower level of aggregation.[d] The services examined were identical with those used for the New York State analysis—elementary and secondary education, welfare, police, and fire. Welfare is a county responsibility; education, police, and fire are administered by the City of Syracuse.

Welfare service was subdivided into six component programs. Given the results of the foregoing attempts to separate quality changes from productivity, only method II, the identification of changes in quality proxies, was attempted. Table 6-3 reports the results.

Education

The major reason for the increase in educational expenditure was the increase in cost. Workload, defined as enrollment, actually fell between 1959 and 1969. Quality-productivity accounts for 48.1 percent of the increase in expenditure for education.

A number of possible quality proxies are available for education. One is the teacher/pupil ratio. This ratio increased between 1959 and 1969, indicating an

[d]Onondaga County had a 1970 population of 472,746. Syracuse, the central city, had a population of 197,208.

Table 6-3

The Sources of Increase in Local Government Expenditure, Onondaga County, 1959-69, Selected Functions[a]

	Change in Expenditure 1959-69	Percentage Change in Expenditure 1959-69	Percentage Change in Expenditure Attributable to		
			Workload	Cost	Quality-Productivity
Education	$14,970,292	113.5	−1.9	53.8	48.1
Welfare					
Home Relief	1,816,783	103.9	60.8	37.5	1.7
Old-Age Assistance	691,030	98.0	−50.3	28.9	121.4
Aid for Dependent Children	14,215,941	514.6	61.8	8.3	30.0
Aid to the Blind	7,340	19.1	−338.7	134.8	303.9
Aid to the Disabled	348,491	159.9	−7.2	18.8	88.4
Child Welfare	2,628,233	215.7	16.6	21.0	62.5
Medical Assistance	13,722,287	383.0	72.7	19.8	8.1
Police	3,033,052	106.0	−9.1	64.4	44.7
Fire	2,954,002	101.2	33.0	88.1	−21.2

[a]See Appendix B for data sources.

increase in the quality of education in Syracuse. Although, particularly in large cities, test scores are of questionable value as quality proxies, they are still often used. The Iowa Test of Basic Skills for reading was administered by the City schools in both 1959 and 1969 for grades 3-9. In 1959 the City average was above the national norm for all grades tested except the ninth grade. In the ninth grade, the City average was 0.1 percent below the national norm. The average scores in 1969 for Syracuse were below the national norm for all grades tested. For the ninth grade, the Syracuse average was 0.83 below the national norm. These test scores indicate a decline in the quality of education in grades 3-9 for the City as compared to national averages.

During the period 1966 and 1970, the Syracuse school system administered a pupil evaluation test in reading for grades 3, 6, and 9. The results of this test indicate the percentage of pupils below "minimum competence" as defined by the Syracuse Board of Education. From 1966 to 1969, the percentage of pupils below minimum competence increased in all grades. This increase again indicates a decline in the quality of education.

There is another way in which these test scores may be interpreted. In 1966, 25 percent of the third grade pupils were below minimum competence in reading. Three years later, in the sixth grade, 39 percent of pupils were below minimum competence. These data indicate an increase in the percentage of pupils below minimum competence between the third and sixth grades. In 1966, 27 percent of pupils in the sixth grade were below minimum competence, while in 1969, in the ninth grade, 28 percent of this group was below minimum competence, indicating a very slight drop in the quality of education between the sixth and the ninth grades.

Taken as a whole, these quality proxies indicate a slight deterioration in the quality of education in Syracuse public schools between 1959 and 1969. The positive residual coupled with quality deterioration suggests a decline in the productivity of the Syracuse school system's provision of education.

Welfare

The welfare service for Onondaga County is broken down by category of expenditure. The categories include all public assistance programs, child welfare, and medical assistance. The positive quality-productivity component for each of the welfare categories indicates either an increase in quality or a decline in productivity in each of these welfare services. In general, welfare coverage in Onondaga County increased over the period. This suggests an increase in the quality of the overall welfare service. The ratio of assisted persons per case worker increased for all public assistance from 136.1 to 160.2 per welfare case worker over the period, suggesting a decline in service quality.[e] Only in the child welfare category did the ratio of recipients to case workers decline over the period.

Between 1959 and 1969 the Onondaga County Social Services Department began to computerize some of its operations. The installation of the computer should have increased both the productivity of the Department by allowing records to be kept more efficiently and the quality of the service by allowing the Department to respond more rapidly to the needs of recipients. The only positive indication of any improvement is that administrative cost declined in all welfare categories, but there is a difficulty in interpreting this decline. It may be the result of computerization and therefore indicate greater productivity. Or it may simply reflect the increase in the recipient/caseworker ratio, suggesting a drop in quality.

An examination of the individual welfare categories yields some additional insight into quality-productivity changes in welfare services. In the three smallest programs—old age assistance, aid to the blind, and aid to the disabled—the majority of the increase in expenditure is attributable to an increase in quality-productivity. In each of these three programs, the number of persons receiving assistance fell while expenditure increased. The overall result was an increase in the dollar amount received per person. Thus the major reason for the

---

[e]This assumes, again, that fewer cases for each caseworker improves the quality of social service.

increase in expenditure was an increase in the quality of the service provided in these three categories.

In the case of child welfare, changes in quality-productivity account for 62.4 percent of the increase in expenditure. In this category, the number of recipient children increased and cases per case worker fell. Both of these findings suggest that at least a part of the change in child welfare expenditure attributable to quality-productivity is a result of an increase in the quality of this service.

Home relief, medical assistance, and aid for dependent children are the three most important welfare categories in terms of both total spending and total number of persons covered. For home relief and medical assistance, very little of the change in expenditure is accounted for by changes in quality-productivity. Increases in workload account for the largest part of the increase in expenditure. Table 6-3 indicates that changes in quality and productivity have not had a significant effect on expenditure in these two categories.

The major portion of the change in expenditure for aid for dependent children is also attributable to increased workload. But in this category, almost 30 percent of the expenditure increase is a result of changes in quality and productivity. Certainly the coverage of this program has improved and to that extent its quality has improved. But the average recipient has enjoyed little if any improvement. From 1959 to 1969, the average recipient received an increase of only $200 ($20 annual average) in real terms. This figure indicates only very slight quality improvement for those who were in this category over the entire period.

Old age assistance, aid to the blind, aid to the disabled, and child welfare all seem to have experienced some improvement in quality. These improvements may account for that part of the change in expenditure attributable to changes in quality-productivity in these categories. For home relief and medical assistance, very little of the change in expenditure is accounted for by quality-productivity changes. Aid for dependent children may have had some quality increase, but there is also the possibility of a decline in the productivity of providing this service for the County.

Police

Increases in cost accounted for 64.4 percent of the increase in police expenditure in the City of Syracuse between 1959 and 1969. The problems involved in defining workload for police were discussed above; since workload is measured by population, there is a decline for Syracuse. The quality-productivity component accounted for 44.7 percent of the increase in police expenditure.

The number of policemen per person was the major quality proxy used in examining the six largest cities in New York State. Applying this proxy to the Syracuse police service suggests an increase in quality.

Other quality proxies may also be employed. One possibility is the ratio of civilian police employees per policeman. An increase in this ratio suggests an increase in the quality of police service. More civilian employees provide each policeman with a larger backup staff and deploys more policemen on the street. For Syracuse, this ratio increased from 0.28 to 0.34 civilian employees per policeman, suggesting an increase in the quality of police service.

The training of the police recruit has increased over the period from ninety hours in 1959 to ten weeks in 1969. This additional training should also provide better policing. New reporting and mapping procedures were introduced such that crime trends can be more easily spotted and additional patrols or procedural changes may be made to adjust for changing crime patterns. Finally, the addition of the police science program during the period helped to improve the education of the policeman. By 1969, twenty-nine police officers had received Associate Degrees in Police Science and another twenty-seven were attending Onondaga Community College to complete the degree. All of these proxies indicate some increase in the quality of police service in Syracuse. Thus at least a part of the increase in expenditure attributable to changes in quality-productivity can be attributed to increases in the quality of the police function.

Fire Protection

Like police, the major reason for the increase in expenditure for fire protection was the increase in cost. Cost increases accounted for 88.1 percent of the increase in expenditures. Increased workload (equalized property values) accounted for another 33.0 percent. Thus, for the fire service, the quality-productivity category declined.

Quality proxies for fire are particularly difficult to interpret. One possible proxy is the ratio of the population to firemen. For the city of Syracuse, this ratio has fallen slightly. This suggests a slight improvement in quality. Another possible proxy is the "key rate." For Syracuse, this rate increased by $0.01 over the period, indicating a slight quality decline. These two quality proxies suggest a very small quality change. Certainly, they do not account for the −21.15 percent of the change in expenditure that is attributed to quality-productivity.

It may be concluded that there is a strong possibility that the productivity of the fire service in Syracuse has improved. Although by 1971, 56 percent of the fire equipment in Syracuse was at least sixteen years old, 44 percent of the equipment that has been replaced since World War II has been more efficient. For example, most new fire trucks purchased since 1959 have been Diesel-powered. This equipment is more economical to use and better for heavy-duty use. This improvement should yield an improvement in productivity. Thus it seems reasonable to argue that the −21.15 percent of increased expenditure attributable to changes in quality-productivity may be accounted for by increases in productivity in the fire service.

Review of Results

The examination of the four government service functions in Onondaga County and Syracuse yields differing results. The productivity of providing education within Syracuse appears to have fallen. The quality of the smaller, relatively unimportant welfare services has increased. For the larger welfare categories—home relief, medical assistance, and aid for dependent children—quality per recipient has improved only slightly in Onondaga County, but coverage has been broadened.

It may be concluded, on the basis of this empirical examination of selected New York State local government services and comparable services for Onondaga County and Syracuse that the measurement of cost, workload, and quality-productivity is a practicable approach to the analysis of local government activities over time.

The findings are not particularly cheerful—there is little strong evidence of major improvements in productivity, except in the provision of fire protection. There is evidence of quality improvement in some service provision, but such improvement is not startling. The findings are therefore in general agreement with the empirical work of Bradford, Malt, and Oates.[1] They are also in agreement with the tentative findings of the Urban Institute for police crime control.[2]

As a technique for analysis of the sources of change in local government expenditure, the approach used here is promising. It isolates cost and workload. It requires that attention be directed to quality and productivity proxies, which means that analysts and local government officials must be continuously concerned with a range of measures that provide insights into the nature of their production functions and their outputs.

7

The Outlook for an Operational Approach

In the United States in the mid-seventies, it is reasonable to anticipate that the state-local public sector will continue to grow, both absolutely in terms of expenditures and relatively as a proportion of total economic activity. Thus it can be expected that citizen-taxpayers will continue to be concerned about government service provision. The quality, cost, and efficiency of such provision will persist as a significant political issue.

This volume has two objectives. The first is to survey the "state of the art" with respect to the measurement of public sector productivity, including an examination of the conceptual linkages between private sector and public sector productivity measures. This survey includes an examination of the empirical work that has been done in this area at all levels of government—federal, state, and local.

The second objective is the development of an operational technique for the measurement of local government productivity changes. The cost, workload, quality-productivity approach provides the framework for such measurement.

The major obstacle encountered in the analysis of local government productivity is the absence of knowledge about public sector production functions. A public sector production function may be conceptualized as consisting of an input vector, an activity vector, an output vector and a consequences vector. The input vector may be mapped through the activities vector, or production function, into a vector of outputs. This vector of outputs along with any other influences, including both other government outputs and environmental factors, may then be mapped indirectly into a vector of consequences.[1]

Measuring output by measuring input, as is done in the national income and product accounts, will not, of course, yield a measure of productivity changes; productivity measures must depend on ratios of inputs to outputs.

Direct outputs appear to be the most appropriate method for estimating quantities of public sector services for productivity analysis. The consequences method ignores the intermediate step, the direct output. Yet it is this step that production theory is built upon. And it has been the analysis of this intermediate step that has provided a great deal of insight into the production process in the private sector.

For certain types of public sector analysis, it may be appropriate to move to consequences and possibly even to develop a consequences function—a general relationship between direct outputs and consequences. It is, after all, the changes in social states which the citizen perceives as government activity. But, apart from some work on social indicators, measuring perceptions of social states has remained outside the economist's domain. Ultimately, the measurement of social states is a necessary goal. But for productivity measurement, using consequences to estimate output largely negates the entire production theory upon which such measurement is founded.

The cost, workload, productivity-quality model is intended to bring the analysis a bit closer to the framework of production functions. The model, developed in Chapter 5 and tested in Chapter 6, is not without its limitations, as has been previously emphasized. The major limitations are (1) the necessary assumption of a linear homogeneous production function, (2) the difficulties in selecting appropriate measures of cost and workload, and (3) the difficulties in interpreting the residual, that is, in separating quality changes in government service provision from productivity changes. The latter problem is in part a matter of value judgment; it is continuously necessary for the analyst to search out the goals and objectives of a government program and then to search for proxy measures of such goals and objectives.

It should be stressed that the model developed in Chapters 5 and 6 is not a tautology. Rather, it hypothesizes that there is a functional relationship among expenditures, the cost of inputs, workload, quality, and productivity. Its use is intended to provide a framework for a systematic exploration of this relationship, function by function and jurisdiction by jurisdiction. This exploration will be most effective at the level where programs are administered. The application of this technique by local government budget officers, or analysts who work with budget officers, should, over time, contribute to a much better understanding of the provision of local government services.

The technique would appear to be less useful for aggregating across jurisdictional lines. A statewide measure of changes in productivity in the provision of welfare or in the provision of elementary and secondary education may comprehend too much diversity for meaningful averaging. And the state of the art has not yet progressed to the point where a national measure of local government productivity changes would have validity.

The responsibility for improvements in local government productivity and in the quality of local government services rests heavily on local government budget officers. And such officers must have adequate backing from elected officials who are seriously interested in such improvement.

With the acceptance of such responsibility, implementation depends very much on the quantity and quality of data that can be gathered and analyzed. Many local governments simply do not collect the data necessary for analysis. Those that do do not usually collect it in a form which is compatible with the data collected by other governmental units. One of the reasons for this state of affairs may be that data collection is not politically charismatic. Few politicians have been reelected because they improved the data-collection system.

The creation of state-local data banks is one possible method for solving this problem. A cooperative banking operation could institutionalize a systematic data reporting network. A federal commission on local government data collection and reporting would also be most useful in coordinating state-local data banks and in reviewing both the form and consistency of the information collected.

Research on government productivity is just beginning. The proper questions may not yet have been asked. Discussion is beginning to move from political rhetoric to academic inquiry to operating experience. Obviously, much is left to be done. The Urban Institute's recommendation for a massive, concentrated two- or three-year study of local government productivity most certainly should be heeded, although even this effort would provide only a beginning foundation for future research.

As research continues and data-gathering improves, the area of technological innovation should not be neglected. There are three aspects of this problem. The first is the basic research and development that must be done to provide the necessary technological and managerial innovations for improving local government productivity. The second is the need for a transfer mechanism.[2] The federal government has taken some interest in the basic R & D work, but much of what it has done has not been transferred to local governments. The third aspect is an implementation mechanism for introducing innovations once they have been developed.

Both state and local governments have expended notoriously little money for research and development. Thus much of this work will have to be done by the federal government. State-local regional productivity councils may be an acceptable device for solving the other two problems. These councils should be staffed and funded by the states and should be composed of locally elected officials and local government employees. Their purpose would be to identify new innovations and encourage implementation of new techniques to improve productivity. Experimentation is necessary, but experimental failures are political catastrophes. Few elected officials are willing to engage in such risky ventures. For an outside source, the council, a failure could be tolerated. Thus such councils could prove to be a most useful mechanism for improving local government productivity.

Answers to taxpayer questions about what is received for tax dollars requires a good information system. Such a system must necessarily include both efficiency and effectiveness measures. Measuring productivity in itself will not solve the problems of local government inefficiency. But measurement will point in the right direction for changes in local government service delivery; it will lead to the development of more effective public services. The thrust of recent productivity analysis has been directed toward activities rather than direct outputs. The methodology emphasized in this volume stresses direct outputs. By concentrating on a specific service, it provides a disaggregated view of the public sector. It does not preclude activity measurement. Rather, it identifies areas of priority concern where analysis is necessary. And in the process it helps to explain the behavior of the local public sector.

There is currently an increased concern about the "quality of life"; such discussion usually centers on how we should all work to improve it. Most thoughtful persons who are concerned about the quality of life are not thinking of color television, a $35,000 house, and two cars for every American family. They are instead thinking of the educational needs of a democratic, mass society, of the whole spectrum of environmental concerns, and of the cultural and spiritual life of the average American. It is not the consumer products of American industry that these concerned citizens wish to distribute more widely. They ask the question that John Ruskin, when he turned from art to social criticism, asked of the political economists of his day:

No one has been bold or clear-sighted enough to put and press home this radical question: what is indeed the noblest tone and reach of life for men; and how can the possibility of it be extended to the greatest numbers?[3]

Officials of the public sector at all levels of government, because their responsibility is to serve the public, are inherently the custodians of this quality of life. Whether they serve well or ill, efficiently or inefficiently, matters very much. Their "outputs" are perishable, as Adam Smith explained, but it is obvious that their products do have value, due in part to their function as custodians.

Productivity measurements will hopefully contribute in a small but not unimportant way to answering Ruskin's provocative question. Public service goes beyond Smith's characterizations of its honorableness and its usefulness; it is absolutely essential. Therefore it is likewise essential for us to be able to measure and evaluate.

Appendixes

Appendix A: Data Sources for Table 6-1

Public Schools

Expenditure. Current operating expenditure from Tables 1-G, 1-H, and 1-I– "Trends in Local Government Statistics, Fiscal Years 1959 through 1969." *Special Report on Municipal Affairs* (Albany: State Comptroller, State of New York, Legislative Document Number 95, 1970), pp. 19, 20, 21.

Workload. Public school enrollment from Table 8, "Fall Enrollment and Average Daily Attendance in Public Elementary and Secondary Schools, 1945-46 to 1968-69." *Annual Education Summary Nineteen Sixty Eight-Sixty Nine. Statistical and Financial Summary of Education in New York State for the Year ending June 30, 1969* (Albany: University of the State of New York, State Education Department, Information Center on Education), p. 11.

Cost. Average starting salary, without fringe benefits, for a new teacher with a B.A.–for 1959, *Teachers' Salary Schedules for 1958-59*, Public Education Research Bulletin (Albany: New York State Teachers Association, vol. 21, no. 3, 1959). For 1969, *Teachers Salary Schedules 1968-69, State Salary Schedule Summary* (Albany: New York State Teachers Association, 1969). The data for New York City for 1969 is from *Facts and Figures 1968-69* (New York: Board of Education, New York City Public Schools).

Quality Proxies for Education. Number of instructional personnel from *Public Employment in 1959 and 1969*, Bureau of the Census, Government Employment/Series GE59 and GE69–no. 1 (Washington, ·D.C.: U.S. Government Printing Office, 1970). Average salary of instructional personnel from *Public Employment*.

Welfare

Expenditure. Expenditures, including local administration, for old-age assistance, aid to dependent children, assistance to the blind, aid to the disabled, home relief, and medical assistance for the needy: for 1959, from Table 1, "Expenditures in State-Aided Locally Administered Public Welfare Programs, 1958 and 1959," *New York State Social Statistics, Statistical Supplement to the Annual Report for 1959*, Annual Report of the New York State Department of Social Welfare, Legislative Document (1960) no. 101, (Albany: Board of Social Welfare, Department of Social Welfare, Bureau of Research and Statistics, 1960),

131

p. 9. For 1969, the data are from *Expenditures for Public Welfare Programs Subject to both Federal and State Aid or to State Aid Only*, New York State, 1969 (Albany: New York State Department of Social Services, 1970), p. 22.

Workload. Number of persons receiving old-age assistance, aid to dependent children, assistance to the blind, aid to the disabled, home relief, and medical assistance for the needy. For 1959, the data source is the same as for expenditures, p. 10. For 1969, the data source is the same as for expenditure, p. 22.

Cost.

$$\frac{C1969}{C1959} = 1 + (a*CPI + b*S + c*MCI)$$

where *CPI* is the percentage change in the consumer price index taken from Table C-45 of the *Economic Report of the President*, 1970 (Washington, D.C.: United States Government Printing Office, 1970), p. 229. *S* is the percentage change in starting salaries from a letter dated June 11, 1971, from the State of New York, Department of Social Services, Albany, N.Y. *MCI* is the percentage change in the medical care component of the consumer price index from Table C-45 of the *Economic Report of the President*, ibid., p. 229. The weights, *a, b,* and *c* are: *a*—the average percentage of total expenditures attributable to all public assistance payments except medical care; *b*—average percentage of expenditure attributable to local administration; and *c*—the average percentage of expenditure attributable to medical payments. $a + b + c = 1$.

Welfare Proxies for Quality. Number of welfare workers from *Public Employment in 1959 and 1969*, Bureau of the Census, Government Employment/Series GE59 and GE69—no. 1 (Washington, D.C.: U.S. Government Printing Office). Average salary of welfare workers from *Public Employment*. Number of persons under the poverty line from Council of Economic Advisers, State of New York.

Police

Expenditure. Current expenditures for police in the six largest cities in New York State from "Part A—Descriptive Characteristics and Revenue, *Comparison of Revenues, Expenditures and Debt: 1949-1959*. Comptroller's Studies in Local Finance, no. 1 (Albany: New York State Department of Audit and Control, 1969). For 1969, unpublished data, Department of Audit and Control.

Workload. Population for each of the six largest cities for 1960 and 1970, from

1970 Census of Population Advance Report, Final Population Counts, New York (Bureau of the Census, Series PC (VI)-34 (Washington, D.C.: U.S. Government Printing Office).

Cost. Percentage change in starting salary, including all fringe benefits except retirement, for each of the six largest cities. In this case, the weights are determined by the percentage of total expenditure spent by each city. The base salary for 1959 is from Table XVII–"Police Department Data for Cities over 10,000," *The Municipal Year Book, 1960* (Chicago: International City Managers' Association, 1960), pp. 398-400. For 1969, the data for the basic salaries is from Table IX–"Police Department Salaries and Expenditures," *The Municipal Year Book, 1970* (Washington, D.C.: International City Management Association, 1970), pp. 300-305. The value of the fringe benefits for New York City and for Syracuse was obtained from their respective city budget offices. The percentage of benefits to basic salary for Syracuse was applied to the other four cities.

Police Quality Proxy. Number of persons per policeman. The number of policemen is from *The Municipal Year Book*, ibid., 1960 and 1970.

Fire

Expenditure. Current expenditures for fire in the six largest cities in New York State. The source is the same as that for police expenditures.

Workload. Full valuation of taxable real property. For 1959, "Part A–Descriptive Characteristics and Revenue," *Comparison of Revenues, Expenditures and Debt: 1949-1959.* Comptroller's Studies in Local Finance, no. 1 (Albany: New York State Department of Audit and Control 1961). For 1969, Table 3–"City Finances, Fiscal Years Ended in 1969," *Special Report on Municipal Affairs*, Legislative Document no. 95 (Albany: State Comptroller, State of New York, 1970).

Cost. The source is the same as cost for police.

Fire Quality Proxy. Number of persons per fireman. The source is the same as that for policemen.

Appendix B: Data Sources
for Table 6-3

Public Schools

Expenditures. Current operating expenditure for Syracuse public schools for the years 1959-60 and 1969-70: for 1959-60, the data is from Table 53, "Expenditures by Major Category in Public Schools, 1959-60," *Annual Educational Summary, New York State, 1959-60* (Albany: State Education Department, Bureau of Statistical Services, 1961), p. 142. For 1969-70, the data is from the *Annual Financial Report* (Syracuse: Syracuse City School District, June 30, 1970).

Workload. Public school enrollment from Table 51, "Public School Enrollment by Grade from Census and Enrollment Reports, Fall 1959," *Annual Educational Summary, New York State, 1959-60* (Albany: State Education Department, Bureau of Statistical Services, September 1969), p. 108. For 1969-70, the data is from Research Report 2-70, *Syracuse Public School Enrollment of 26 September 1969*, Research Department (Syracuse: City School District, 1969).

Cost.

$$\frac{C_{1969}}{C_{1959}} = 1 + (a*S + b*CPI)$$

where S is the percentage change in the starting salary, including fringe benefits, for a starting teacher with a B.A. This information is from "Teachers Salary Schedule" (Syracuse: City School District, July 1, 1959, and September 1, 1969). The value of fringe benefits is based on estimates by Julius Deuble, Administrative Staff Director, Syracuse City School System. The *CPI* is the percentage change in the consumer price index from Table C-45 of the *Economic Report of the President* (Washington: Government Printing Office, 1970), p. 229. The weights, a and b are: a—the average percentage of total expenditure attributable to salaries; b—the average percentage of all other expenditure. ($a + b = 1$.)

Quality Proxies for Education. The number of teachers and average teacher salaries from the *Annual Budget of the City of Syracuse* for 1959 and 1969, September 29, 1958, pp. 55-69, and October 26, 1968, pp. 180-200. Test scores are from Sandy Rudin, Research Assistant, Research Department, City School District, Syracuse, New York. Discussions with both Julius Deuble and Sandy Rudin were very helpful in preparing this section. Neither is responsible for the conclusions about quality and productivity.

Welfare

Expenditure. Expenditure by program, including local administrative expenditure: for 1959, the data are from "Annual Report of the Department of Public Welfare, Onondaga County for the Year 1959," *Journal of the Board of Supervisors–Onondaga County 1959*, pp. 367-83. For 1969, the data are from Schedule C, "Annual Report of the Department of Social Services, Onondaga County, 1970" (mimeo).

Workload. Number of persons receiving benefits by category. For 1959, the source is the same as that for expenditure, p. 381. For 1969, the source is the same as that for expenditure, Schedule F.

Cost.

$$\frac{C_{1969}}{C_{1959}} = 1 + (a*CPI + b*S + c*MCI)$$

where *CPI* is the percentage change in the consumer price index (see reference under preceding paragraph, "Cost." *S* is the percentage change in starting salaries, including fringe benefits, for the Onondaga County caseworker. For 1959, the source is the "Appropriation for the Department of Public Welfare," *Journal of the Board of Supervisors–Onondaga County 1959*, pp. 214-220, For 1969, the source is the *Journal of the County Legislature, 1969*, pp. 525-31. The value of fringe benefits is based on estimates provided by William Potter, County Budget Director of Onondaga County. *MCI* is the percentage change in the medical care component of the consumer price index, from Table C-45 of the *Economic Report of the President* (Washington, D.C.: Government Printing Office, 1970), p. 229.

The weights, *a*, *b*, and *c*, are: *a*–the average percentage of total expenditure attributable to each public assistance category (a separate cost index was used for each category); *b*–average percentage of expenditure attributable to local administration for each category; *c*–the average percentage of expenditure attributable to medical payments. *c* is zero in all cases except that of medical assistance. (*a* + *b* + *c* = 1.)

Quality Proxies for Welfare. The sources for these proxies are as listed above and from discussions with Thomas Baker, Director, Accounting Division, Department of Social Services, and William Potter, Budget Director, Onondaga County. Neither Mr. Baker nor Mr. Potter is responsible for the conclusions concerning quality and productivity in this section.

Police

Expenditure. Current expenditure for police in the City of Syracuse: data from "Detailed Statement of Appropriation and Expenditures, Protection of Persons and Property," *Annual Report of the Commissioner of Finance, 1959 and 1969*, pp. 35 and 28 respectively.

Workload. Population for the City of Syracuse, for 1960 and 1970, from *1970 Census of Population Advance Report, Final Population Counts*, New York (Bureau of the Census, Series PC (VI)-34, January 1971).

Cost. Percentage change in starting salaries, including fringe benefits, for the beginning policeman in Syracuse: data for cost is based on estimates provided by the Budget Office, City of Syracuse.

Quality Proxies for Police. Average salaries are from the *Budget of the City of Syracuse*, New York, 1959 and 1969, pp. 33-35 and 120-123 respectively. All other quality proxies are from *Annual Report*, Department of Police, City of Syracuse, 1959 and 1969.
Discussions with Deputy Chief Fred Scharoun and Lt. Hours were most helpful in this part of the report. Neither is responsible for the conclusions concerning quality and productivity in this section.

Fire Protection

Expenditure. Current expenditure for fire protection in the City of Syracuse, including the fire control center data from "Detailed Statement of Appropriations and Expenditures, Protection of Persons and Property," *Annual Report of the Commissioner of Finance, 1959 and 1969*, pp. 35 and 28 respectively.

Workload. Full valuation of taxable real property. For 1959, "Part A—Descriptive Characteristics and Revenue," *Comparison of Revenues, Expenditures and Debt: 1949–1959*. Comptroller's Studies in Local Finance, no. 1 (Albany: New York State Department of Audit and Control, 1961). For 1969, Table 3—"City Finances, Fiscal Years Ended in 1969," *Special Report on Municipal Affairs*, State Comptroller, State of New York, Legislative Document no. 95 (Albany: 1970).

Cost. The source is the same as cost for police.

Quality Proxies for Fire Protection. The average salaries are from the Budget of the City of Syracuse, New York, 1959 and 1969, pp. 35-36 and 112-119 respectively. All other quality proxies are from *Annual Report, Syracuse Fire Department, 1959 and 1969* and from discussions with Fire Chief Thomas F. Hanlon. All conclusions with respect to quality and productivity are the responsibility of the authors.

Notes

Notes

Chapter 1
Introduction

1. In a recent survey of ten large cities, people were asked, "Do people in the city get their money's worth from their local taxes?" In seven of the ten cities, the "no" responses were greater than 50 percent. York Willbern and Lawrence A. Williams, "City Taxes and Services: Citizens Speak Out," *Nation's Cities* 19 (August 1971): 1-32.

2. Edward K. Hamilton, "Productivity: The New York City Approach," *Public Administration Review* 32 (November/December 1972): 785.

3. William J. Baumol, "Macroeconomics of Unbalanced Growth: The Anatomy of Urban Crisis," *American Economic Review* 57 (June 1967): 416.

4. This article brought forth an immediate wave of comments. Many of the commentators felt that Baumol had incorrectly measured service output. See Carolyn Shaw Bell, "Macroeconomics of Unbalanced Growth: Comment," 58 *American Economic Review* (September 1968): 877-884.

5. A.A. Walters, "Production and Cost Functions: An Econometric Survey," *Econometrica* 31 (January-April 1963): 1-26.

6. Adam Smith, *The Wealth of Nations* (New York: Modern Library, 1937), p. 315.

7. Ibid.

Chapter 2
Productivity

1. If the ratio is expressed in terms of physical units or constant money values, it is termed "physical productivity." It may also be expressed as "value productivity" in which case output is in current dollar values and input is in physical units or constant dollars. These two measures should be distinguished from a measure of cost per unit of production. This latter is an input-output ratio. Inputs are measured in current dollars and outputs are measured in physical units. Solomon Fabricant, "Productivity," *International Encyclopedia of Social Science*, vol. 12, David L. Stills, ed. (New York: Macmillan Company and the Free Press, 1968), p. 524.

2. Solomon Fabricant, *Basic Facts on Productivity Change*, Occasional Paper no. 63 (New York: National Bureau of Economic Research, 1959); Fabricant, "Productivity," pp. 523-36; Fabricant, *A Primer on Productivity* (New York: Random House, 1959). Note that this list does not include the numerous measurement studies done by Fabricant.

3. Werner Z. Hirsch, *The Economics of State and Local Government* (New York: McGraw-Hill, 1970), p. 148.

4. U.S. Congress, Joint Economic Committee, *Measuring and Enhancing Productivity in the Federal Sector*, by representatives of the Civil Service Commission, General Accounting Office, and Office of Management and Budget, 92d. Cong., 2d. sess. (Washington, D.C.: U.S. Government Printing Office, 1972), p. 123.

5. For a more complete discussion of production, see William J. Baumol, *Economic Theory and Operations Analysis*, 2nd ed. (Englewood Cliffs, N.J.: Prentice-Hall, 1965), pp. 250-70.

6. Carl F. Christ, "Comment," *Output, Input, and Productivity Measurement, Studies in Income and Wealth*, vol. 25, Conference on Research in Income and Wealth, National Bureau of Economic Research (Princeton: Princeton University Press, 1961), p. 42.

7. Sig Gissler, "Productivity in the Public Sector: A Summary of a Wingspread Symposium," with a preface by Leslie Paffrath, *Public Administration Review* 32 (November/December 1972): 843.

8. Two other measures are sometimes discussed within the general category of effectiveness measurement. The first, termed program efficiency, refers to a cost effectiveness analysis of a particular program. The second, termed policy effectiveness, concerns an evaluation of the effects of an overall policy. Because of the lack of a general theory to support either of these types of measures and due to the large number of variables which must be considered, both of these measures have proved to be extremely difficult to use meaningfully. For a further discussion of both program efficiency and policy effectiveness, see Nestor E. Terleckyj, "Productivity Analysis, Tempered with Judgement, Improves Efficiency," *Defense Management Journal* 8 (October 1972): 25-29.

9. The authors of *Measuring and Enhancing Productivity in the Federal Sector* seem to feel that such a reconciliation can be accomplished quite easily, but they do not explain how one does it. Nor do they explain how effectiveness measures might be incorporated into a theory of production. Such an incorporation is a necessary first step toward a meaningful reconciliation of these two measures. *Measuring and Enhancing Productivity in the Federal Sector*, pp. 123-30.

10. The latter method was developed by Jean Fourastic, *Productivity, Prices, and Wages*, Project no. 235, The European Productivity Agency of the Organization for European Economic Co-operation (Paris, 1957). This method has the advantage of requiring little information and therefore allowing historical comparisons. In developing it, Fourastic assumed that the state of technology solely determines both wages and prices. This assumption, which is only plausible in the long run, and the adjustments which must be made on both wages and price to remove influences such as changes in tax rates, inflation, and so forth, make this method rather questionable. Such a ratio is more a measure

of changes in the level of living than of changes in productivity. For additional criticism, see Roger Grégoire, "Preface," ibid., pp. 5-6.

11. John W. Kendrick, *Productivity Trends in the United States* (Princeton: Princeton University Press, 1961 for the National Bureau of Economic Research).

12. Ibid., p. 3.

13. Ibid., pp. 33-34.

14. Thomas M. Humphrey, "Productivity and Its Measurement," *Federal Reserve Bank of Richmond, Monthly Review* (June 1971): 5. Humphrey's sources for these estimates were Solomon Fabricant, *Basic Facts on Productivity Change* (New York: National Bureau of Economic Research, 1958); Kendrick, *Productivity Trends*; and U.S. Council of Economic Advisers, *Economic Report of the President* (Washington, D.C.: U.S. Government Printing Office, 1971).

15. To gain the flavor of the literature in this area, see Yoram Barzel, "Productivity in the Electric Power Industry, 1929-1955," *Review of Economics and Statistics* 45 (November 1963): 395-408; and Benjamin Slatin, "Measures of Productivity in the Paper and Pulp Industry," *Productivity Measurement Review* (February 1964): 51-61. For a good summary of these types of studies, see U.S. Department of Labor, *Productivity Analysis*, by Benjamin P. Klotz, Staff Paper 3 (Washington, D.C.: U.S. Government Printing Office, 1970).

16. Fabricant, "Productivity," p. 524.

17. Ibid., p. 526.

18. The more important of these studies include Robert M. Solow, "Technical Change and the Aggregate Production Function," *Review of Economics and Statistics* 39 (August 1957): 312-20; Kendrick, *Productivity Trends*; Edward F. Denison, *The Sources of Economic Growth in the United States and the Alternatives before Us*, Supplementary Paper no. 13 (New York: Committee for Economic Development, 1962); Edward F. Denison assisted by Jean-Pierre Poullier, *Why Growth Rates Differ*: Postwar Experience in Nine Western Countries. (Washington, D.C.: Brookings Institution, 1967); D.W. Jorgenson and Z. Griliches, "The Explanation of Productivity Change," *Survey of Current Business* 52 pt II (May 1972): 31-64.

19. Denison, *The Sources of Economic Growth*, pp. 146-50.

20. Jorgenson and Griliches, "Explanation of Productivity Change," p. 272.

21. Although there are a number of criticisms, they tend to fall into these major categories: those who reject the approach on the ground that there is no such thing as an aggregate production function, those who reject the approach on the ground that the theory of income distribution based on marginal productivity does not hold, and finally, those who reject the approach on the ground that the residual really does not tell us anything about economic growth. For an excellent discussion of these criticisms, see *The Residual Factor and Economic Growth* (Paris: Organization for Economic Co-operation and Development, 1964).

22. Joan Robinson, *Essays in the Theory of Economic Growth* (New York: Macmillan, 1963), p. 34.

23. Jorgenson and Griliches, "Explanation of Productivity Change," p. 256.

24. Denison and Poullier, *Why Growth Rates Differ*: Postwar Experience in Nine Western Countries, pp. 14-15. © 1967 by the Brookings Institution, Washington, D.C.

25. Edward F. Denison, "Some Major Issues in Productivity Analysis: An Examination of Estimates by Jorgenson and Griliches," *Survey of Current Business* 52, pt II (May 1972): 38.

26. This point raises conceptual issues that are beyond the scope of this volume. The major point is that the treatment of taxes will affect the results of a productivity index. For more detailed consideration of this point, see Denison, ibid., 40-41.

27. U.S. Department of Labor, Bureau of Labor Statistics, *The Meaning and Measurement of Productivity*, by Jerome A. Mark, Bulletin no. 1714 (Washington, D.C.: U.S. Government Printing Office, 1971), p. 10.

28. For a complete discussion of these weaknesses, see Gardner Ackley, *Macroeconomic Theory* (New York: Macmillan Company, 1961), pp. 31-77.

29. Denison seems to prefer this view. For example, see Edward F. Denison, "The Unimportance of the Embodiment Question," *American Economic Review* 54 (March 1964): 90-93. Kenneth Arrow takes this notion of technological change and develops it into a full-blown growth theory—the theory of learning by doing. For example, see Kenneth J. Arrow, "The Economic Implications of Learning by Doing," *Review of Economic Studies* 29 (June 1962): 155-73.

30. This view is most expressed in the form of vintage models—models of economic growth which rest upon the assumption that technological change is embodied in new capital. For an excellent set of readings supporting this view, see Joseph E. Stiglitz and Hirofumi Uzawa, eds., *Readings in the Modern Theory of Economic Growth* (Cambridge, Massachusetts: The M.I.T. Press, 1969), pp. 156-209.

31. Richard R. Nelson, "Aggregate Production Functions and Medium-Range Growth Projection," *American Economic Review* 54 (September 1964): 593.

32. Ibid., p. 597.

33. D.W. Jorgenson and Z. Griliches, "Issues in Growth Accounting: A Reply to Edward F. Denison," *Survey of Current Business* 52, pt. II (May 1972): 69.

34. Edward F. Denison, "Final Comments," *Survey of Current Business* 52, pt II (May 1972): 98-99.

35. Denison, "Some Major Issues in Productivity Analysis," p. 47.

36. Ibid., 54-58.

37. Mark, *Meaning and Measurement of Productivity*, p. 11.

38. Ibid., p. 9.

39. Ibid., pp. 13-14.

40. Raymond W. Goldsmith, *A Study of Saving in the United States*, 3 vols.

(Princeton: Princeton University Press, 1955-56); and Goldsmith, *The National Wealth of the United States in the Post-war Period* (Princeton: Princeton University Press, 1962).

Chapter 3
Public Sector Output

1. Jerome A. Mark, "Progress in Measuring Productivity in Government," *Monthly Labor Review* 95 (December 1972): 5.

2. John Kenneth Galbraith, *The Affluent Society* (Boston: Houghton Mifflin, 1957).

3. U.S. Department of Labor, Bureau of Labor Statistics, *The Theory of Hedonic Quality Measurement and Its Use in Price Indexes*, by Jack E. Triplett, Staff Paper 6 (Washington, D.C.: U.S. Government Printing Office, 1971).

4. Kenneth J. Arrow, *Social Choice and Individual Values* (New York: John Wiley, 1963).

5. Werner Z. Hirsch, *The Economics of State and Local Government* (New York: McGraw-Hill Book Company, 1970), pp. 745-51.

6. Raymond W. Goldsmith, *The National Wealth of the United States in the Postwar Period* (Princeton: Princeton University Press, 1962), pp. 209-10.

7. Jesse Burkhead and Jerry Miner, *Public Expenditure* (Chicago: Aldine-Atherton, 1971), p. 301.

8. Victor R. Fuchs and Jean Alexander Wilburn, *Productivity Differences within the Service Sector*, Occasional Paper 102 (New York: Columbia University Press, National Bureau of Economic Research, 1967); and Victor R. Fuchs, *The Service Economy* (New York: Columbia University Press, National Bureau of Economic Research, 1968).

9. Fuchs, *Service Economy*, p. 100.

10. Ibid., pp. 99-107.

11. Ibid., pp. 107-14.

12. Carolyn Shaw Bell, "Macroeconomics of Unbalanced Growth: Comment," *The American Economic Review* 58 (September 1968): 877-84. Baumol has countered this argument by suggesting that Bell's example is a "beautiful" illustration of the growth of amateur activity in the service area. This growth is the consequence of high prices for professional services. These higher prices, according to Baumol, are the result of the slow rate of productivity increase in services. The increase in amateur activity implies a reduction in the quality of the service, not an increase in its productivity. William J. Baumol, "Macroeconomics of Unbalanced Growth: Comment," *American Economic Review* 58 (September 1968): 896-97.

13. Fuchs, *Service Economy*, pp. 115-25.

14. Ibid., pp. 117-18.

15. Determining exactly which proxies to use, how to weight those proxies to reflect their relative importance, and how to adjust them for changes in quality constitute major problems. Almost every proponent of this method has his own scheme for solving each of these three problems. For a summary of the different possible schemes, see ibid., pp. 118-26.

16. A more detailed discussion of the problems associated with measuring the cost of hospital care can be found in Martin S. Feldstein, *The Rising Cost of Hospital Care* (Washington, D.C.: Information Resources Press, 1971).

17. Fuchs, *The Service Economy*, p. 43.

18. Ibid., pp. 4-5.

19. Richard A. Musgrave, "Comments," *Issues in Urban Economics*, Harvey S. Perloff and Lowdon Wingo, eds. (Baltimore, Maryland: Johns Hopkins Press, 1968), p. 572.

20. Jesse Burkhead, Thomas G. Fox, and John W. Holland, *Input and Output in Large-City High Schools* (Syracuse, New York: Syracuse University Press, 1967).

21. Hirsch, *Economics of State and Local Government*, pp. 154-55.

22. Carl S. Shoup, *Public Finance* (Chicago: Aldine, 1969), pp. 79-143.

23. Seymour Sacks and David C. Ranney, "Suburban Education: A Fiscal Analysis," *Educating an Urban Population*, Marilyn Gittell, ed. (Beverly Hills, California: Sage Publications, 1967), p. 62.

24. For a summary of the studies using this type of analysis prior to 1968, see Roy Bahl, "Studies on Determinants of Public Expenditures: A Review," in *Functional Federalism: Grants-in-Aid and PPB Systems*, Selma J. Mushkin and John F. Cotton, eds. (Washington, D.C.: State-Local Finances Project of the George Washington University, 1968), pp. 184-207. Also see Burkhead and Miner, *Public Expenditure*, pp. 304-17.

25. Some have even suggested that changes in quality proxies be used to estimate changes in output quantities. See Hirsch, *Economics of State and Local Government*, pp. 152-54.

26. Lancaster's theory originally appeared in two articles: Kelvin J. Lancaster, "A New Approach to Consumer Theory," *The Journal of Political Economy* 74 (April 1966): 132-57, and Lancaster, "Allocation and Distribution Theory: Technological Innovation and Progress," *American Economic Review* 56 (May 1966): 14-23. It was developed and expanded in Lancaster, *Consumer Demand: A New Approach* (New York: Columbia University Press, 1971).

27. Lancaster, "Allocation and Distribution Theory," p. 14.

28. Ibid., p. 14.

29. Ibid. Even though Lancaster's approach is quite interesting, it may not be as new as he would lead one to believe. A body of literature exists on hedonic indexes. These indexes basically interpret Lancaster's characteristics as quality indicators. Triplett sees Lancaster's work as an extension of the work on hedonic indexes and criticizes Lancaster for neglecting to include mention of this

literature in his "new approach." Jack Triplett, "Book Review," *Journal of Economic Literature* 11 (March 1973): 77-81.

30. Burkhead and Miner, *Public Expenditure*, p. 304.

31. Ibid., p. 177.

32. For an excellent discussion of PPBS, see Joint Economic Committee, Subcommittee on Economy in Government, *The Analysis and Evaluation of Public Expenditures: The PPB System* volumes I, II, and III, 91st Cong., 1st sess. (Washington, D.C.: U.S. Government Printing Office, 1969). Many of the papers that appear in this work have been reprinted in *Public Expenditures and Policy Analysis*, Robert H. Haveman and Julius Margolis, eds. (Chicago: Markham Publishing Company, 1970).

33. Burkhead and Miner, *Public Expenditure*, p. 175.

34. Robert N. Grosse, "Problems of Resource Allocation in Health," *The Analysis and Evaluation of Public Expenditures: The PPB System*, vol. III, p. 1219.

35. Ibid., p. 1220.

36. Robert H. Haveman, "Introduction," *Public Expenditures and Policy Analysis*, p. 7.

37. Ibid., p. 8.

38. D.F. Bradford, R.A. Malt, and W.E. Oates, "The Rising Cost of Local Public Services: Some Evidence and Reflections," *National Tax Journal* 22 (June 1969): 185-202.

39. Ibid., p. 186.

40. Ibid., pp. 186-87.

41. Ibid., p. 187.

42. Ibid., p. 188.

43. Hirsch, *Economics of State and Local Government*, p. 156.

44. Werner Z. Hirsch, "The Supply of Urban Services," *Issues in Urban Economics*, Harvey S. Perloff and Lowdon Wingo, eds. (Baltimore, Maryland: Johns Hopkins Press, 1968), p. 486.

45. Ibid., p. 495.

46. Hirsch, *Economics of State and Local Government*, pp. 154-55.

47. Ibid., p. 154.

48. Ibid.

49. Burkhead, Fox, and Holland, *Input and Output in Large-City High Schools*; for a review of similar studies, see Harvey A. Averch, Stephen J. Carroll, Theodore S. Donaldson, Herbert J. Kiesling and John Pincus, *How Effective Is Schooling* (Santa Monica, California: RAND Corporation, 1972).

50. Ibid., p. 24.

51. Ibid., p. 34.

52. Ibid.

53. Shoup, *Public Finance*, pp. 79-143.

Chapter 4
Empirical Studies

1. Solomon Fabricant, *The Trend of Government Activity in the United States since 1900* (New York: National Bureau of Economic Research, 1952), pp. 84-111.

2. Ibid., pp. 100-101.

3. William J. Baumol, "Macroeconomics of Unbalanced Growth: The Anatomy of Urban Crisis," *American Economic Review* 57 (June 1967): 415-26. This model is reviewed above in Chapter 1.

4. U.S. Congress, Joint Economic Committee, *Measuring and Enhancing Productivity in the Federal Sector*, by representatives of the Civil Service Commission, General Accounting Office, and Office of Management and Budget, Joint Committee Print, 92d. Cong., 2d. sess. (Washington, D.C.: U.S. Government Printing Office, 1972), p. 15.

5. For discussion of these output criteria, see Joint Office of Management and Budget, Civil Service Commission, General Accounting Office Project, *Federal Productivity: Methods, Measurements, and Results; A Staff Study to Determine the Feasibility of Developing Productivity Indices for the Federal Sector* (August 1972), pp. 16, 28, and 58. This study is hereafter referred to as *Federal Productivity*.

6. Executive Office of the President, Bureau of the Budget, *Measuring Productivity of Federal Government Organizations* (Washington, D.C.: U.S. Government Printing Office, 1964).

7. Ibid., p. 128. Algebraically, this process is as follows: output units x (man-years divided by output units) = man years or weighted output.

8. U.S. Department of Labor, Bureau of Labor Statistics, *Technological Changes and Employment in the United States Postal Service* (Witt Bowden), Bulletin no. 574 (Washington, D.C.: U.S. Government Printing Office, 1932).

9. Witt Bowden, "Technological Changes and Employment in the United States Postal Service," *Monthly Labor Review* 35 (October 1932): 745-50.

10. For an example of one possible linking adjustment method, see *Federal Productivity*, pp. 181-83.

11. Bowden, "Technological Changes," p. 751.

12. Ibid., pp. 755-59.

13. Ibid., p. 747.

14. William A. Vogely, *A Case Study in the Measurement of Government Output* (Santa Monica, California: RAND Corporation, 1958).

15. Ibid., p. 271.

16. Henry D. Lytton, "Recent Productivity Trends in the Federal Government: An Exploratory Study," *The Review of Economics and Statistics* 41 (November 1959): 341-59.

17. Ibid., pp. 355-57.

18. Ibid., p. 343.

19. Ibid.

20. Ibid., p. 354.

21. At this conference, John W. Kendrick developed the concept of "organization productivity." This concept was extensively referred to in the BOB's 1964 study, but seems to have been dropped, in name if not in practice, in the more recent studies of federal government productivity. Executive Office of the President, Bureau of the Budget, "Measuring the Productivity of Organizations," John W. Kendrick, *Progress in Measuring Work*, Management Bulletin (Washington, D.C.: U.S. Government Printing Office, 1962), pp. 8-20.

22. Executive Office of the President, Bureau of the Budget, *Measuring Productivity of Federal Government Organizations* (Washington, D.C.: U.S. Government Printing Office, 1964).

23. For a discussion of the difficulties encountered by the Bureau of Land Management, see ibid., pp. 299-362.

24. Ibid., pp. 131, 168.

25. Ibid., pp. 45, 186.

26. Ibid., p. 15.

27. The petroleum pipeline industry was the only major private-sector industry to grow at a faster rate. For the period 1958-69, it had an average annual rate of growth of 10.0 percent. For other comparisons, see Table 2-1, Chapter 2.

28. *Measuring Productivity of Federal Government Organizations*, p. 4.

29. Nestor E. Terleckyj, "Recent Trends in Output and Input of the Federal Government," *American Statistical Association, 1964 Proceedings of the Business and Economic Statistics Section* (December 1964): 76-94.

30. Ibid., p. 88.

31. *Measuring and Enhancing Productivity in the Federal Sector*, p. 72.

32. Ibid., pp. 2-5.

33. *Federal Productivity*, p. 16. For a complete listing of original elements, outputs, and output definitions, see pp. 67-160.

34. Ibid., p. 20. It is interesting to note that one of the grounds for rejection was extreme fluctuation. Such rejection is not statistically valid, but is a basis for further examination.

35. Ibid., pp. 20-24.

36. Ibid., pp. 28-29.

37. For an example of the actual adjustment, see ibid., pp. 179-84.

38. *Federal Productivity*, pp. 30-32.

39. *Measuring and Enhancing Productivity in the Federal Sector*, pp. 113-14.

40. Ibid., pp. 22-23.

41. *Federal Productivity*, pp. 14-15.

42. Ibid., pp. 36-38.

43. *Measuring and Enhancing Productivity in the Federal Sector*, p. 27.

44. *Federal Productivity*, pp. 39-42.

45. Ibid., p. 48.

46. Ibid., pp. 46-47.

47. *Measuring and Enhancing Productivity in the Federal Sector*, pp. 28-30. The results of the other parts of phase II are interesting but not relevant to this inquiry. For a summary of these recommendations, see ibid., pp. 72-78. One recommendation relating to productivity measurement is for the establishment of a "productivity bank" to finance federal government capital investments. Aside from its other advantages, such a bank would help to facilitate estimates of public capital depreciation. For a summary of the discussion of such a bank, see ibid., pp. 63-64 and 131-35.

48. For examples, see Peter G. Peterson, "Productivity in Government and the American Economy," *Public Administration Review* 32 (November/December 1972): 740-47; Jerome A. Mark, "Meanings and Measures of Productivity," *Public Administration Review* 32 (November/December 1972): 747-53; and John W. Kendrick, "Public Capital Expenditures and Budgeting for Productivity Advances," *Public Administration Review* 32 (November/December 1972): 804-807.

49. For examples, see Thomas D. Morris, William H. Corbett, and Brian L. Usilaner, "Productivity Measures in the Federal Government," *Public Administration Review* 32 (November/December 1972): 753-63; and Thomas D. Morris, "Joint Study Shows Productivity Gains," *Defense Management Journal* 8 (October 1973): 16-20.

50. For examples, see Frederick C. Thayer, "Productivity: Taylorism Revisited (Round Three)," *Public Administration Review* 32 (November/December 1972): 833-40; Sig Gissler, "Productivity in the Public Sector: A Summary of a Wingspread Symposium," *Public Administration Review* 32 (November/December 1972): 840-50; and Nestor E. Terleckyj, "Productivity Analysis, Tempered with Judgment, Improves Efficiency," *Defense Management Journal* 8 (October 1973): 25-28.

51. U.S. Bureau of the Census, *Statistical Abstract of the United States: 1972*, (Washington, D.C.: 1972), pp. 259, 402.

52. *Federal Productivity*, pp. 132-33.

53. Ibid., p. 28.

54. *Measuring and Enhancing Productivity in the Federal Sector*, p. 28.

55. Ibid., p. 23.

56. For examples, see Richard S. Frank, "Economic Report/Productivity Commission Studies Techniques to Improve Public-Sector Output," *National Journal* (June 10, 1972): 998-1004; "The Push to Boost Government Productivity," *Business Week* (May 13, 1972): 160-64; and Dan Cordtz, "City Hall Discovers Productivity," *Fortune* (October 1971): 93-128.

57. Harry P. Hatry and Donald M. Fisk, *Improving Productivity and Productivity Measurement in Local Governments*, Prepared for the National Commission on Productivity (Washington, D.C.: Urban Institute, 1971), pp. 35-46.

58. Clarence E. Ridley and Herbert A. Simon, *Measuring Municipal Activities* (Chicago: International City Managers' Association, 1938).

59. Ibid., p. 14.

60. Ibid.

61. Ibid., pp. 13-14.

62. Henry J. Schmandt and G. Ross Stephens, "Measuring Municipal Output," *National Tax Journal* 13 (December 1960): 369-75.

63. Bertram M. Gross, *The Managing of Organizations*, vol. II (New York: Free Press of Glencoe, 1964), pp. 602-606.

64. These studies have been primarily cross-sectional of single functions within the framework of determinants analysis. Their primary concern has been to examine whether or not economies of scale exist. On the whole, the results have been inconclusive. The studies are useful in that they provide some insight into those factors affecting the cost of local government services, but they do not attempt to estimate changes in productivity. For a review of these studies, see Werner Z. Hirsch, *The Economics of State and Local Government* (New York: McGraw-Hill, 1970), pp. 167-84.

65. D.F. Bradford, R.A. Malt, and W.E. Oates, "The Rising Cost of Local Public Services: Some Evidence and Reflections," *National Tax Journal* 22 (June 1969): 185-202. For a review of the concept of D-output, see Chapter 3.

66. Ibid., p. 191.

67. Ibid., p. 202.

68. The Urban Institute and the International City Management Association, *The Challenge of Productivity Diversity: Part I, Overall Summary and Recommendations*; Urban Institute, *The Challenge of Productivity Diversity: Part II, Measuring Solid Waste Collection Productivity*; Urban Institute, *The Challenge of Productivity Diversity, Part III, Measuring Police-Crime Control Productivity*; and Urban Institute and the *International City Management Association, The Challenge of Productivity Diversity: Part IV, Procedures for Identifying and Evaluating Innovations—Six Case Studies*, all prepared for the National Commission on Productivity (Washington, D.C.: Urban Institute, 1972).

69. The Urban Institute and the International City Management Association, *The Challenge of Productivity Diversity: Part I*, ibid., p. 2.

70. Harry P. Hatry and Donald M. Fisk, *Improving Productivity and Productivity Measurement in Local Governments*, prepared for the National Commission on Productivity (Washington, D.C.: Urban Institute, 1971), p. 3.

71. The Urban Institute, *The Challenge of Productivity Diversity: Part II*, pp. 41-49. The method for developing the sample survey is discussed in some detail in Louis H. Blair and Alfred I. Schwartz, *How Clean is Our City?* (Washington, D.C.: Urban Institute, 1972).

72. The Urban Institute, *The Challenge of Productivity Diversity: Part III*, pp. 43-79.

73. Edward K. Hamilton, "Productivity: The New York City Approach," *Public Administration Review* 32 (November/December 1972): 784-95.

74. The Urban Institute and the International City Management Association, *The Challenge of Productivity Diversity: Part IV*.

75. Patrick J. Lucey, "Wisconsin's Productivity Policy," *Public Administration Review* 32 (November/December 1972): 795-99.

76. Ralph C. Bledsoe, Dennis R. Denny, Charles D. Hobbs, and Raymond S. Long, "Productivity Management in the California Social Services Program," *Public Administration Review* 32 (November/December 1972): 799-807.

Chapter 5
Measuring Changes in Local
Government Expenditure

1. Werner Z. Hirsch, *Analysis of the Rising Costs of Public Education*, Joint Economic Committee (Washington, D.C.: U.S. Government Printing Office, 1959).

2. Dick Netzer, "State-Local Finance in the Next Decade," *Revenue Sharing and Its Alternatives: What Future for Fiscal Federalism?* Joint Economic Committee (Washington: U.S. Government Printing Office, 1967), vol. III, p. 1344.

3. Lawrence R. Kegan and George P. Roniger, "The Outlook for State and Local Finance," *Fiscal Issues on the Future of Federalism*, Supplementary Paper no. 23 (New York: Committee for Economic Development, 1968), pp. 231-83.

4. Selma J. Mushkin and Gabrielle C. Lupo, "Project '70: Projecting the State-Local Sector," *Review of Economics and Statistics* 49 (May 1967): 237-45; "State and Local Finances Projections: Another Dimension?" *Southern Economic Journal* 33 (January 1967): 426-29.

5. Selma J. Mushkin and Gabrielle Lupo, "Is There a Conservative Bias in State-Local Sector Expenditure Projections?" *National Tax Journal* 20 (September 1967): 282-91.

6. William H. Robinson, "Financing State and Local Governments: The Outlook for 1975," New York Chapter of the American Statistical Association, April 24, 1969 (unpublished).

7. Charles L. Schultze, Edward R. Fried, Alice M. Rivlin, and Nancy H. Teeters, eds., *Setting National Priorities, the 1972 Budget* (Washington, D.C.: Brookings Institution, 1971), pp. 134-57; and Robert D. Reischauer, "The State and Local Fiscal Crisis in Perspective" (Washington, D.C.: Brookings Institution, 1971), pp. 1-41 (unpublished).

8. Reischauer, ibid., p. 35.

9. Andrew F. Brimmer, "Inflation, Private Spending, and the Provision of Public Services," 171st Commencement Exercises of Middlebury College, Middlebury, Vermont, May 30, 1971, pp. 1-20. The statistical appendix is attributed to Paul Schneiderman of the FRB staff and the methodology is attributed to Reischauer.

10. Council of Economic Advisers, State of New York, *Annual Report* (Albany, 1972), p. 20.

11. Werner Z. Hirsch, *The Economics of State and Local Government* (New York: McGraw-Hill, 1970), pp. 179-84.

12. The residual component R_t corresponds roughly to the "scope and quality" factor use in previous studies.

13. For a discussion of this technique for indexing costs in the public sector, see Jerry Miner, *Social and Economic Factors in Spending for Public Education* (Syracuse, New York: Syracuse University Press, 1963), pp. 73-84.

14. See, for example, Alan K. Campbell and Seymour Sacks, *Metropolitan America* (New York: Free Press, 1967), esp. Chapters 2 and 5; Roy W. Bahl, Jr., and Robert Saunders, "Determinants of Changes in State and Local Government Expenditures," *National Tax Journal* 18 (March 1965): 50-57.

15. D.R. Bradford, R.A. Malt, and W.E. Oates, "The Rising Cost of Local Public Services: Some Evidence and Reflections," *National Tax Journal* 22 (June 1969): 185-202.

Chapter 6
Cost, Workload, Quality, and Productivity

1. D.F. Bradford, R.A. Malt, and W.E. Oates, "The Rising Cost of Local Public Services: Some Evidence and Reflections," *National Tax Journal* 22 (June 1969): 185-202.

2. The Urban Institute, *The Challenge of Productivity Diversity: Part II, Measuring Police-Crime Control Productivity*, prepared for the National Commission on Productivity (Washington, D.C.: Urban Institute, 1972).

Chapter 7
The Outlook for an Operational Approach

1. Bradford, Malt, and Oates provide an excellent discussion of the concept of mapping a vector of inputs through a production function to yield a vector of outputs. But unfortunately, they do not discuss the nature of that production function. D.F. Bradford, R.A. Malt, and W.E. Oates, "The Rising Cost of Local Public Services: Some Evidence and Reflections," *National Tax Journal* 22 (June 1969): 185-202.

2. For a review of some of the work in this area, see *Nation's Cities* 10 (July 1972): entire issue.

3. E.T. Cook and Alexander Wedderburn, eds., *The Works of John Ruskin: Modern Painters*, vol. 7 (London and New York: Library Edition, 1903-1913), p. 430.

Bibliography

Bibliography

Books

Blair, Louis H., and Schwartz, Alfred I. *How Clean Is Our City*. Washington, D.C.: Urban Institute, 1972.

Burkhead, Jesse, and Miner, Jerry. *Public Expenditure*. Chicago: Aldine-Atherton, 1971.

＿＿＿＿, with Thomas G. Fox and John W. Holland. *Input and Output in Large-City High Schools*. Syracuse, N.Y.: Syracuse University Press, 1967.

Campbell, Alan K., and Sacks, Seymour. *Metropolitan America*. New York: Free Press, 1967.

Denison, Edward F. *The Sources of Economic Growth in the United States and the Alternatives before Us*. Supplementary Paper no. 13. New York: Committee for Economic Development, 1962.

＿＿＿＿. *Why Growth Rates Differ*. Washington, D.C.: Brookings Institution, 1967.

Fabricant, Solomon. *A Primer on Productivity*. New York: Random House, 1969.

＿＿＿＿. *Basic Facts on Productivity Change*. Occasional Paper 63. New York: National Bureau of Economic Research, 1959.

＿＿＿＿. *The Trend of Government Activity in the United States since 1900*. New York: National Bureau of Economic Research, 1952.

Feldstein, Martin S. *The Rising Cost of Hospital Care*. Washington, D.C.: Information Resources Press, 1971.

Fiscal Outlook for State and Local Government to 1975. New York: Tax Foundation, 1966.

Fourastic, Jean. *Productivity, Prices, and Wages*. Project no. 235. Paris: The European Productivity Agency of the Organization for European Economic Co-operation, 1957.

Fuchs, Victor R., ed. *Production and Productivity in the Service Industries, Studies in Income and Wealth*. Vol. 34. New York: National Bureau of Economic Research, 1969.

＿＿＿＿. *The Service Economy*. National Bureau of Economic Research. New York: Columbia University Press, 1968.

＿＿＿＿, and Wilburn, Jean Alexander. *Productivity Differences within the Service Sector*. Occasional Paper 102. National Bureau of Economic Research. New York: Columbia University Press, 1967.

Goldsmith, Raymond W. *A Study of Saving in the United States*. Vols. I, II, and III. Princeton, New Jersey: Princeton University Press, 1955-56.

＿＿＿＿. *The National Wealth of the United States in the Postwar Period*. Princeton, New Jersey: Princeton University Press, 1962.

Gross, Bertram M. *The Managing of Organizations*. Vol. II. New York: Free Press of Glencoe, 1964.

Hatry, Harry, and Fisk, Donald M. *Improving Productivity and Productivity Measurement in Local Government*. Prepared for the National Commission on Productivity. Washington, D.C.: Urban Institute, 1971.

Haveman, Robert H., and Margolis, Julius, eds. *Public Expenditures and Policy Analysis*. Chicago: Markham Publishing Company, 1970.

Hirsch, Werner Z. *The Economics of State and Local Government*. New York: McGraw-Hill, 1970.

Kendrick, John W. *Productivity Trends in the United States*. Princeton, N.J.: Princeton University Press for the National Bureau of Economic Research, 1961.

Lancaster, Kelvin J. *Consumer Demand: A New Approach*. New York: Columbia University Press, 1971.

Margolis, Julius, ed. *The Analysis of Public Output*. New York: National Bureau of Economic Research, 1970.

Miner, Jerry. *Social and Economic Factors in Spending for Public Education*. Syracuse, N.Y.: Syracuse University Press, 1963.

National Bureau of Economic Research. *Output, Input and Productivity Measurement, Studies in Income and Wealth*. Vol. 25. New York: NBER, 1961.

Organization for Economic Co-operation and Development. *The Residual Factor and Economic Growth*. Paris: OECD, 1964.

Ridley, Clarence E., and Simon, Herbert A. *Measuring Municipal Activity*. Chicago: International City Managers' Association, 1938.

Schultze, Charles L.; Fried, Edward R.; Rivlin, Alice M.; and Teeters, Nancy H. *Setting National Priorities, the 1972 Budget*. Washington, D.C.: Brookings Institution, 1972.

Shoup, Carl S. *Public Finance*. Chicago: Aldine Publishing Company, 1969.

Stiglitz, Joseph E., and Uzawa, Hirofumi, eds. *Readings in the Modern Theory of Economic Growth*. Cambridge, Mass.: M.I.T. Press, 1969.

The Urban Institute. *The Challenge of Productivity Diversity*. Parts I, II, III, and IV. Prepared for the National Commission on Productivity. Washington, D.C.: Urban Institute, 1972.

Vogely, William A. *A Case Study in the Management of Government Output*. Research Memorandum RM-1934-RC. Santa Monica, Calif.: RAND Corporation, 1958.

Wasserman, William. *Education Price and Quantity Indexes*. Syracuse, N.Y.: Syracuse University Press, 1963.

Webb, Kenneth, and Hatry, Harry. *Obtaining Citizen Feedback*. Washington, D.C.: Urban Institute, 1973.

Articles

Abramovitz, Moses. "Economic Growth in the United States: A Review Article." *American Economic Review* 62 (September 1962): 762-82.

Arrow, Kenneth J. "The Economic Implications of Learning by Doing." *Review of Economic Studies* 29 (June 1962): 155-73.

Bahl, Roy. "Studies on Determinants of Public Expenditures: A Review." *Functional Federalism: Grants-in-Aid and PPB Systems.* Selma J. Mushkin and John F. Cotton, eds., Washington, D.C.: State-Local Finances Project of the George Washington University, 1968, pp. 184-207.

_____ , and Saunders, Robert. "Determinants of Change in State and Local Government Expenditures." *National Tax Journal* 18 (March 1965): 50-57.

Barzel, Yoram. "Productivity in the Electric Power Industry, 1929-1955." *Review of Economics and Statistics* 45 (November 1963): 395-408.

Baumol, William J. "Macroeconomics of Unbalanced Growth: Comment." *American Economic Review* 58 (September 1968): 896-97.

_____ . "Macroeconomics of Unbalanced Growth: The Anatomy of Urban Crisis." *American Economic Review* 57 (June 1967): 415-26.

Bell, Carolyn Shaw. "Macroeconomics of Unbalanced Growth: Comment." *American Economic Review* 58 (September 1968): 877-84.

Bledsoe, Ralph L.; Denny, Dennis R.; Hobbs, Charles D.; and Long, Raymond S. "Productivity Management in the California Social Services Program." *Public Administration Review* 32 (November/December 1972): 799-807.

Bowden, Witt. "Technological Changes and Employment in the United States Postal Service." *Monthly Labor Review* 35 (October 1932): 745-50.

Bradford, D.F.; Malt, R.A.; and Oates, W.E. "The Rising Cost of Local Public Services: Some Evidence and Reflections." *National Tax Journal* 22 (June 1969): 185-202.

Christ, Carl F. "Comment." *Output, Input, and Productivity Measurement, Studies in Income and Wealth.* Vol. 25. National Bureau of Economic Research. Princeton, N.J.: Princeton University Press, 1961, pp. 41-43.

Cordtz, Dan. "City Hall Discovers Productivity." *Fortune* (October 1971): 93-128.

Denison, Edward F. "Classification of Sources of Growth." *The Review of Income and Wealth* 18, no. 1. (March 1972): 1-26.

_____ . "Final Comments." *Survey of Current Business* 52, pt II (May 1972): 95-110.

_____ . "Some Major Issues in Productivity Analysis: An Explanation of Estimates by Jorgenson and Griliches." *Survey of Current Business* 52, pt II (May 1972): 37-63.

_____ . "The Unimportance of the Embodiment Question." *American Economic Review* 64 (March 1964): 90-93.

Fabricant, Solomon. "Productivity." *International Encyclopedia of Social Science.* David L. Stills, ed. Vol. 12, New York: Macmillan Company and the Free Press, 1968, pp. 523-35.

Frank, Richard S. "Economic Report/Productivity Commission Studies Techniques to Improve Public-Sector Output." *National Journal* (June 10, 1972): 998-1004.

Gissler, Sig. "Productivity in the Public Sector: A Summary of a Wingspread

Symposium." Preface by Leslie Paffrath. *Public Administration Review* 32 (November/December 1972): 840-50.

Grosse, Robert N. "Problems of Resource Allocation in Health." *The Analysis and Evaluation of Public Expenditures: The PPS System.* Vol. III. Washington, D.C.: U.S. Government Printing Office, 1969, pp. 1197-1223.

Hamilton, Edward M. "Productivity: The New York City Approach." *Public Administration Review* 32 (November/December 1972): 784-95.

Hirsch, Werner Z. "The Supply of Urban Public Services." *Issues in Urban Economics.* Harvey S. Perloff and Lowdon Wingo, eds. Baltimore: Johns Hopkins Press, 1968, pp. 477-525.

Humphrey, Thomas M. "Productivity and Its Measurement." *Federal Reserve Bank of Richmond, Monthly Review* (June 1971): 2-10.

Jorgenson, D.W., and Griliches, Zvi. "Issues in Growth Accounting: A Reply to Edward F. Denison." *Survey of Current Business* 52, pt II (May 1972): 65-94.

_____ , and Griliches, Zvi. "The Explanation of Productivity Change." *The Review of Economics and Statistics* 34 (July 1967): 249-82.

Kegan, Lawrence R., and Roniger, George P. "The Outlook for State and Local Finance." *Fiscal Issues in the Future of Federalism.* Supplementary Paper 23. New York: Committee for Economic Development, 1968, pp. 231-83.

Kendrick, John W. "Public Capital Expenditures and Budgeting for Productivity Advances." *Public Administration Review* 32 (November/December 1972): 804-807.

Lancaster, Kelvin J. "A New Approach to Consumer Theory." *The Journal of Political Economy* 74 (April 1966): 132-57.

_____ . "Allocation and Distribution Theory: Technological Innovation and Progess." *American Economic Review* 56 (May 1966): 14-23.

Lucey, Patrick J. "Wisconsin's Productivity Policy." *Public Administration Review* 32 (November/December 1972): 795-99.

Lytton, Henry D. "Recent Productivity Trends in the Federal Government: An Exploratory Study." *Review of Economics and Statistics* 41 (November 1959): 341-59.

Margolis, Julius. "The Demand for Urban Public Services." *Issues in Urban Economics.* Harvey S. Perloff and Lowdon Wingo, eds., Baltimore, Md,: Johns Hopkins Press, 1968, pp. 527-64.

Mark, Jerome A. "Meanings and Measures of Productivity." *Public Administration Review* 32 (November/December 1972): 747-53.

_____ . "Progress in Measuring Productivity in Government." *Monthly Labor Review* 45 (December 1972): 3-6.

Morris, Thomas D. "Joint Study Shows Productivity Gains." *Defense Management Journal* 8 (October 1972): 16-20.

_____ , William H. Corbett, and Brian L. Usilaner. "Productivity Measures in the Federal Government." *Public Administration Review* 32 (November/December 1972): 753-63.

Musgrave, Richard A. "Comments." *Issues in Urban Economics*. Harvey S. Perloff and Lowdon Wingo, eds., Baltimore: Johns Hopkins Press, 1968, pp. 567-74.

Mushkin, Selma J., and Lupo, Gabrielle C. "Is There a Conservative Bias in State-Local Sector Expenditure Projections?" *National Tax Journal* 20 (September 1967): 282-291.

_____, and Lupo, Gabrielle C. "Project '70: Projecting the State-Local Sector." *Review of Economics and Statistics* 49 (May 1967): 237-45.

_____, and Lupo, Gabrielle C. "State and Local Finances Projections: Another Dimension?" *Southern Economic Journal* 33 (January 1967): 426-29.

Nation's Cities 7, no. 10 (July 1972).

Nelson, Richard R. "Aggregate Production Functions and Medium-Range Growth Projections." *American Economic Review* 54 (September 1964): 575-606.

Peterson, Peter G. "Productivity in Government and the American Economy." *Public Administration Review* 32 (November/December 1972): 740-47.

Sacks, Seymour, and Ranney, David L. "Suburban Education: A Fiscal Analysis." *Educating an Urban Society*. Marilyn Gittell, ed., Beverly Hills, Calif.: Sage Publications, 1967, pp. 60-76.

Schmandt, Henry J., and Stephens, G. Ross. "Measuring Municipal Output." *National Tax Journal* 13 (December 1960): 369-75.

Slatin, Benjamin. "Measures of Productivity in the Paper and Pulp Industry." *Productivity Measurement Review* (February 1964): 51-61.

Solow, Robert M. "Technical Change and the Aggregate Production Function." *Review of Economics and Statistics* 39 (August 1957): 312-20.

Terleckyj, Nestor E. "Productivity Analysis, Tempered with Judgment, Improves Efficiency." *Defense Journal* 8 (October 1972): 25-29.

Thayer, Frederick C. "Productivity: Taylorism Revisited (Round Three)." *Public Administration Review* 32 (November/December 1972): 833-40.

Triplett, Jack. "Book Review." *Journal of Economic Literature* 11 (March 1973): 77-81.

Walters, A.A. "Production and Cost Functions: An Econometric Survey." *Econometrica* 31 (January-April 1963): 1-26.

Walzer, Norman. "An Illinois Municipal Price Index and Its Meaning." *Illinois Municipal Review* (August 1969): 4-7.

_____. "A Price Index for Municipal Purchases." *National Tax Journal* 23 (December 1970): 441-47.

_____. "Municipal Expenditure Patterns in Illinois." *Illinois Municipal Review* (February 1970): 10-12.

Willbern, York, and Williams, Lawrence A. "City Taxes and Services: Citizens Speak Out." *Nation's Cities* 9 (August 1971): 1-32.

Federal Government Publications

Executive Office of the President. Bureau of the Budget. *Measuring Productivity of Federal Government Organizations*. Washington, D.C.: U.S. Government Printing Office, 1964.

Executive Office of the President. Bureau of the Budget. "Measuring the Productivity of Organizations." *Progress in Measuring Work*. Management Bulletin. Washington, D.C.: U.S. Government Printing Office, 1962, pp. 8-20.

Joint Office of Management and Budget, Civil Service Commission, and General Accounting Office Project. *Federal Productivity; Methods, Measurements, Results, A Staff Study to Determine the Feasibility of Developing Productivity Indices for the Federal Sector*. Washington, D.C.: U.S. Government Printing Office, 1972.

U.S. Congress. Joint Economic Committee. *Analysis of the Rising Cost of Public Education*, Werner Z. Hirsch. 86th Cong., 1st sess. Washington, D.C.: U.S. Government Printing Office, 1959.

U.S. Congress. Joint Economic Committee. Hearings, Subcommittee on Priorities and Economy in Government. *Federal Productivity*, 93rd Cong., 1st sess. Washington, D.C.: U.S. Government Printing Office, 1974.

U.S. Congress. Joint Economic Committee. *Measuring and Enhancing Productivity in the Federal Sector*, representatives of the Civil Service Commission, General Accounting Office, and Office of Management and Budget. Joint Economic Committee. 92d. Cong., 2d sess. Washington, D.C.: U.S. Government Printing Office, 1972.

U.S. Congress. Joint Economic Committee. Subcommittee on Economies in Government. *The Analysis and Evaluation of Public Expenditures: The PPB System*. Volumes I, II, and III. 91st Cong., 1st sess. Washington, D.C.: U.S. Government Printing Office, 1969.

U.S. Congress. Joint Economic Committee. "State-Local Finance in the Next Decade," Dick Netzer. *Revenue Sharing and Its Alternatives: What Future for Fiscal Federalism?* Vol. II. 90th Cong., 1st sess. Washington, D.C.: U.S. Government Printing Office, 1967, pp. 1336-49.

U.S. Department of Labor. *Productivity Analysis*, Benjamin P. Klotz. Staff Paper no. 3. Washington, D.C.: U.S. Government Printing Office, 1970.

U.S. Department of Labor. Bureau of Labor Statistics. "Concepts and Measures of Productivity," Jerome A. Mark. *The Meaning and Measurement of Productivity*. Bulletin no. 1714. Washington, D.C.: U.S. Government Printing Office, 1971, pp. 7-15.

U.S. Department of Labor. Bureau of Labor Statistics. *Indexes of Output per Man-Hour, Selected Industries 1939 and 1947-70*. Bulletin 1692. Washington, D.C.: U.S. Government Printing Office, 1971.

U.S. Department of Labor. Bureau of Labor Statistics. "The Meaning of Productivity," Herbert Stein. *The Meaning and Measurement of Productivity*.

Bulletin no. 1714. Washington, D.C.: U.S. Government Printing Office, 1971, pp. 1-5.

U.S. Department of Labor. Bureau of Labor Statistics. *Productivity: A Bibliography*. Bulletin no. 1514. Washington, D.C.: U.S. Government Printing Office, 1966.

U.S. Department of Labor. Bureau of Labor Statistics. *Technological Changes and Employment in the United States Postal Service*, by Witt Bowden. Bulletin no. 574. Washington, D.C.: U.S. Government Printing Office, 1932.

U.S. Department of Labor. Bureau of Labor Statistics. *The Theory of Hedonic Quality Measurement and Its Use in Price Indexes*, Jack E. Triplett. Staff Paper 6. Washington, D.C.: U.S. Government Printing Office, 1971.

Other

Brimmer, Andrew F. "Inflation, Private Spending, and the Provision of Public Services." Remarks presented at the 171st Commencement Exercises of Middlebury College, Middlebury, Vermont, May 30, 1971.

Dawson, John E. "Measuring Outputs as a Basis of Public Budgeting." Ph.D. dissertation, Syracuse University, 1971.

Kendrick, John. *Postwar Productivity Trends in the United States, 1948-1969*. New York: National Bureau of Economic Research, MS.

New York State. Council of Economic Advisers. "Explanation and Data Sources for Table 6." Unpublished memorandum.

Reischauer, Robert D. "The State and Local Fiscal Crisis in Perspective." Washington, D.C.: Brookings Institution, February 25, 1971, unpublished memorandum.

Robinson, William H. "Financing State and Local Governments: The Outlook for 1975." Paper presented at the Eleventh Annual Forecasting Conference, New York Chapter of the American Statistical Association, April 24, 1969.

Index

Index

About the Authors

John P. Ross is an assistant professor in the Division of Environmental and Urban Systems at Virginia Polytechnic Institute and State University. He received the Ph.D. from Syracuse University in 1973 and taught in the Department of Economics of Central Michigan University. He has also served as Deputy Director of the Ohio Commission on Local Government Services.

Jesse Burkhead is Maxwell Professor of Economics at Syracuse University; he has also taught at Lehigh University and has served as a consultant to numerous government agencies and foundations. He received the B.A. from Carleton College, the M.A. and Ph.D. from the University of Wisconsin, and the M.P.A. from Harvard University. Professor Burkhead is the author of *Government Budgeting* (Wiley, 1956), *State and Local Taxes for Public Education* (Syracuse University Press, 1963), and *Public School Finance: Economics and Politics* (Syracuse University Press, 1964); he is coauthor of *Public Expenditure* (Aldine, 1971).

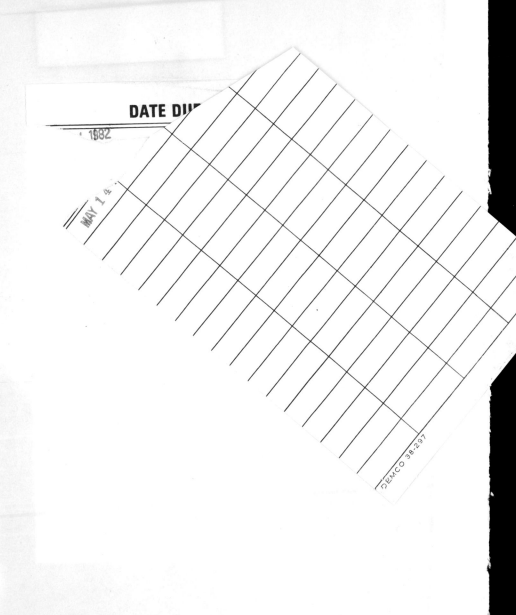